Christmas

Published by Augsburg Publishing House

Christmas

An American Annual of Christmas Literature & Art

VOLUME FIVE
FIFTH EDITION

Edited by Randolph E. Haugan

Published by Augsburg Publishing House Minneapolis

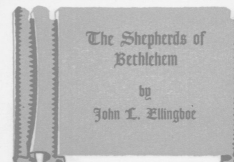

The Shepherds of
Bethlehem

by
John L. Ellingboe

THE SONG OF THE SHEPHERDS

haste, O people: all are bidden—
haste from places high or hidden:
In Mary's Child the kingdom comes,
　　the heaven in beauty bends!
he has made all life completer:
he has made the Plain Way sweeter,
For the stall is his first shelter and
　　the cattle his first friends.

he has come! the skies are telling:
he has quit the glorious dwelling;
And first the tidings came to us,
　　the humble shepherd folk.
he has come to field and manger,
And no more is God a Stranger:
he comes as Common Man at home
　　with cart and crooked yoke.

As the shadow of a cedar
To a traveler in Gray Kedar
Will be the kingdom of his love,
　　the kingdom without end.
Tongues and ages may disclaim him,
Yet the heaven of heavens will name him
Lord of peoples, Light of nations,
　　elder Brother, tender Friend.

The Song of the
Shepherds

by

Edwin Markham

All Praise to Him

A Christmas Carol
by
James E. Freeman

Music by J. S. Bach
arranged by
Stanley Avery

1. All praise to him whose love is told, In story that shall ne'er grow old, Un-til the stars of light are cold, The Christ of Ma-ry born. He comes to take the form of man, An age-less Son whose

2. With low-ly mien, he comes to earth, No splen-dor marks His hum-ble birth; A man-ger the mer-ry price-less worth, 'Tis here a God is born. The an-gels chant their mu-sic glad some song. While shepherds on the

3. Through-out the earth, in eve-ry clime, From earl-iest dawn to lat-est time. We ring the Christ-mas chime, The silv-'ry bells of peace. O let their mu-sic still re-sound, And spread a-broad the

Table of Contents

Volume Five

"Christmas" Articles

"Christmas" Stories

"Christmas" Carols

"Christmas" Illustrators

Lois Lenski
Knute Heldner
R. J. Norman
John L. Ellingboe
Regina Koelnau
Ludwig Koelnau
Andrea del Sarto
Pompeo Girolamo Batoni
Frederigo Barocci
Herschel C. Logan
Norm Deer
David Workman
Traus
Arthur Nelson
Byron Robertson

"Christmas" Poetry

Selected by Thomas Curtis Clark

"Christmas" Photography

Manufactured in the United States of America

And It Came to Pass

THE GOSPEL STORY OF THE FIRST CHRISTMAS

Illustration by R. J. Norman

AND it came to pass in those days, that there went out a decree from Cæsar Augustus, that all the world should be taxed. (And this taxing was first made when Cyrenius was governor of Syria.) And all went to be taxed, every one into his own city. And Joseph also went up from Galilee, out of the city of Nazareth, into Judæa, unto the city of David, which is called Bethlehem; (because he was of the house and lineage of David:) to be taxed with Mary his espoused wife, being great with child. And so it was, that, while they were there, the days were accomplished that she should be delivered. And she brought forth her firstborn Son, and wrapped Him in swaddling clothes, and laid Him in a manger; because there was no room for them in the inn.

THE VISIT OF THE ANGELS

AND there were in the same country shepherds abiding in the field, keeping watch over their flock by night. And, lo, the angel of the Lord came upon them, and the glory of the Lord shone round about them: and they were sore afraid. And the angel said unto them, Fear not: for, behold, I bring you good tidings of great joy, which shall be to all people. For unto you is born this day in the city of David a Saviour, which is Christ the Lord. And this shall be a sign unto you; Ye shall find the Babe wrapped in swaddling clothes, lying in a manger. And suddenly there was with the angel a multitude of the heavenly host praising God, and saying,

Glory to God in the highest,
and on earth peace, good-will
toward men.

THE VISIT OF THE SHEPHERDS

AND it came to pass, as the angels were gone away from them into heaven, the shepherds said one to another, Let us now go even unto Bethlehem, and see this thing which is come to pass, which the Lord hath made known unto us. And they came with haste, and found Mary, and Joseph, and the Babe lying in a manger. And when they had seen it, they made known abroad the saying which was told them concerning this Child. And all they that heard it wondered at those things which were told them by the shepherds. But Mary kept all these things, and pondered them in her heart. And the shepherds returned, glorifying and praising God for all the things that they had heard and seen, as it was told unto them.

THE VISIT OF THE WISE MEN

NOW when Jesus was born in Bethlehem of Judæa in the days of Herod the king, behold, there came wise men from the East to Jerusalem, saying, Where is He that is born King of the Jews? For we have seen His star in the East, and are come to worship Him. When Herod the king had heard these things, he was troubled, and all Jerusalem with him. And when he had gathered all the chief priests and scribes of the people together, he demanded of them where Christ should be born. And they said unto him, In Bethlehem of Judæa: for thus it is written by the prophet, And thou Bethlehem, in the land of Juda, art not the least among the princes of Juda: for out of thee

shall come a Governor, that shall rule my people Israel. Then Herod, when he had privily called the wise men, enquired of them diligently what time the star appeared. And he sent them to Bethlehem, and said, Go and search diligently for the young Child; and when ye have found Him, bring me word again, that I may come and worship Him also. When they had heard the king, they departed; and, lo, the star, which they saw in the East, went before them, till it came and stood over where the young Child was. When they saw the star, they rejoiced with exceeding great joy. And when they were come into the house, they saw the young Child with Mary His mother, and fell down, and worshipped Him: and when they had opened their treasures, they presented unto Him gifts; gold, and frankincense, and myrrh. And being warned of God in a dream that they should not return to Herod, they departed into their own country another way.

THE FLIGHT INTO EGYPT

AND when they were departed, behold, the angel of the Lord appeareth to Joseph in a dream, saying, Arise, and take the young Child and His mother, and flee into Egypt, and be thou there until I bring thee word: for Herod will seek the young Child to destroy Him. When he arose, he took the young Child and His mother by night, and departed into Egypt: and was there until the death of Herod: that it might be fulfilled which was spoken of the Lord by the prophet, saying, Out of Egypt have I called my Son. Then Herod, when he saw that he was mocked by the wise men, was exceeding wroth, and sent forth, and slew all the children that were in Bethlehem, and in all the coasts thereof, from two years old and under, according to the time which he had diligently enquired of the wise men. Then was fulfilled that which was spoken by Jeremy the prophet, saying, In Rama was there a voice heard, lamentation, and weeping, and great mourning, Rachel weeping for her children, and would not be comforted, because they are not. But when Herod was dead, behold, an angel of the Lord appeareth in a dream to Joseph in Egypt, saying, Arise, and take the young Child and His mother, and go into the land of Israel: for they are dead which sought the young Child's life. And he arose, and took the young Child and His mother, and came into the land of Israel. But when he heard that Archelaus did reign in Judæa in the room of his father Herod, he was afraid to go thither: notwithstanding, being warned of God in a dream, he turned aside into the parts of Galilee: And he came and dwelt in a city called Nazareth: that it might be fulfilled which was spoken by the prophets, He shall be called a Nazarene.

Kunte Holdner

The Calm of Holy Night

By WILLIAM C. EDGAR

THE village of Falling Water, in the Pleasant Valley, lies under a snowy mantle of white. Looking down upon it from the top of the hill the pathway leads over the footbridge, spanning the narrow gorge through which flows the once musical brook, now frozen and silent.

From its little white houses lights gleam, kindly and hospitably, and slow curls of smoke float gently and almost perpendicularly from their chimneys, for the night is still and windless. Looking afar across the valley of the Shining River, one can see the line of wooded hills, now snowclad, and perched far up and remote on one of them a light shines from the window of a solitary and isolated home, a friendly beacon to its distant neighbors across the frozen river.

Not far from the village itself lies the quiet cemetery in which rest, peacefully and serenely, the forefathers and founders of the settlement and those who have since followed them to their undisturbed slumber on the hillside. One thinks of them, this still, cold night, not as if they were gone and mostly forgotten, but as lying there, warmly wrapped in their blanket of snow, dreamily and contentedly contemplating the peace and glory of the world above them.

ACROSS wide stretches of newly fallen and unbroken snow, from a distant farm yard, comes the lonely bark of a restless watch dog, not alarmingly as if some nocturnal marauder threatened the family peace, but half sleepily, as if, newly and temporarily aroused to a sense of duty, he was perfunctorily resolved to inform the listening world that the household guardian was on the alert against any possible danger.

Far down the winding street appears a small cluster of lights, moving irregularly, and there comes the sound of childish voices singing an old Swedish Christmas hymn. It is a group of the village children on their rounds of carol singing, from house to house, and making their final call.

It behooves these young carolers to make an end to their pilgrimage and tumble into bed, for brief are the hours that remain before it will be time to awaken and go forth again. At five o'clock in the morning, in accordance with an Old World custom, here faithfully observed, the village will be awakened by the sound of the church bell, ringing out over the snow in the frosty, crystalline air.

Candles will be lit in every house and, in obedience to another summons of the bell, forth will troop to church the members, both old and young, of each family. From every street and lane and by-path the faithful will come in the dim light of early morning. Among them will be a few of the very old folk, whom the village ever holds in honor and reverence, some dressed according to ancient fashion, the women wearing shawls about their heads. Staff in hand they will trudge along the snowy pathway to the church in company with the others.

WITH the disappearance of the band of carol singers, silence and the night settle over the village as the moon sinks in the western horizon. The inhabitants have fallen asleep, with the spire of the little church standing out, glistening, over the roof of trees, as a sign that the God in whom the sleepers trust guards them from all harm.

Once again it is the calm and solemn night preceding the birthday of Christ, and for all the thousands of miles that lie between the place of His nativity and this far western spot, and for all the two thousand years that intervene between that day and this, it is possible to imagine that Bethlehem in Judea was even such a village as this and slept even as this does, on the eve of His coming. It is easily possible to imagine His gentle presence in such streets as these, following the streams, walking in the woods, gazing upon its wide river and visiting in its homes; talking to its people, healing its sick and bringing comfort and hope to its sorrowful, bereft and forlorn.

What could be more natural and appropriate to His character and custom than to see Him now, this mystic night, walking in the light of the stars down this deserted village street, bent on an errand of love and mercy?

In such a place as this was Christ born, and He loved the countryside and simple people of good and kindly intent, choosing from them, rather than from the great and the learned, those who were to be His followers and His personal friends.

THIS night the radiant, eloquent heavens and the silent, expectant, receptive earth bear witness to the fundamental verity of the words He uttered and the things He taught, regardless of man's varied and often contradictory interpretation of their meaning.

Which of us, standing alone in the mystery and all-surpassing beauty of such a night, with feet upon a hushed and sleeping world, its strident voices and clamorous contentions stilled; alone with the infinite, unfathomable order, grandeur and splendor of the limitless universe, will dare challenge its obvious meaning with the futile sophistications, speculations and theories of mere men?

Will he not, rather, humbly admit his human inability to solve the meaning and significance of the glory above him, or even, with his finite mind, to advance for it a hypothesis, and so rest his wearied soul in the faith that He who made it all, set it in motion and ordained its course, must be a God of mercy and love, in whose almighty hand rests secure man's fate, both here and hereafter?

THESE glittering and glorious stars, their satellites and constellations, which one can see with the natural eye, are as nothing compared with the number disclosed by the telescope, and these, astronomers tell us, are but a fraction of those that exist in our solar system; furthermore, stretching away into infinity of space are other worlds and systems than ours, uncounted and humanly uncountable.

To some minds the revelations of human science, showing that this world we know is but an insignificant fraction of the universe, have brought disturbance and confusion of thought, and a rude and unwelcome interruption to the placid acceptation of the idea that our world is an exceptional and favored creation and the others beyond are merely ordained to minister to it.

To such the obvious conclusion follows that it cannot possibly concern the great Designer of all and we are, after all, nothing better than incidental atoms in the scheme of things. Therefore they are despairing, almost hopeless, as one whose once secure anchorage is lost. They regret that science has gone so far and lament that it has not gone further and discovered the Impenetrable Reason behind the creation of other worlds than this.

There is, however, a philosophy more hopeful than such a counsel of gloom, which appears to be at least equally logical. If the Creator is great enough and wise enough to order and install such myriads of worlds and systems, all serving His unknown purpose, nothing He has made can be beneath His care and consideration, least of all man whom He has endowed, above all others, with the power of thought and aspiration, and, as most of us believe, with a soul capable of survival beyond its earthly environment.

It matters not that there may be other worlds beyond our present knowledge, or that the meaning, intent and purpose of them be unknown to us; looking up to the heavens on such a night as this, there comes back an unmistakable message of good-will toward men which we would be blind and foolish to misinterpret. Instead of becoming self-deprecatory because of the revelations of human science, we should welcome them and be proud of man's achievement in this direction, taking them as evidence that he was not created merely to eat, drink and perish like the beasts of the field.

SAID the Psalmist, who puzzled over these same questions many years before the coming of Christ:

"O Lord our Lord, how excellent is Thy name in all the earth! Who hast set Thy glory above the heavens.

"When I consider Thy heavens, the work of Thy fingers, the moon and the stars, which Thou hast ordained; what is man, that Thou visitest him.

"For Thou hast made him a little lower than the angels and hast crowned him with glory and honor."

And again the same wise philosopher said:

"The heavens declare the glory of God and the firmament sheweth His handywork.

"Day unto day uttereth speech, and night unto night sheweth knowledge.

"There is no speech nor language where their voice is not heard."

This voice of the heavens, heard in every speech and language universally, can be rightly interpreted only in the reassuring angelic refrain of *Et in terra pax hominibus*.

THE CHRIST CHILD

And will He come tonight,
The Christ Child, stooping low
From where the stars are white?
Kindle the casement light,
*   That He may know*
We watch for Him this night across the snow.

Hush for a little space,
Lest His footfall draw near,
And kneel and pray His grace
Unto a silent place,
*   That we may hear.*
If so His voice might call us low and clear.

Will He but enter there,
The narrow threshold o'er,
As our beloved and share
The lonely fireside where
*   They come no more,*
Lifting His sacred hands while we adore?

The flickering candle trim
Above the darkened street.
Like notes of seraphim
The holy bells ring sweet,
*   The midnight dim*
Waits for the glory: They are calling Him.

—ANNE G. MORSE.

"O LITTLE TOWN OF BETHLEHEM"

"O little town of Bethlehem
*   How still we see thee lie!"*
How mystical thy beauty
*   Beneath that starry sky!*
But, little town, forgotten
*   The dreams that flamed within*
The breast of Him thou gavest
*   To save us from our sin!*

O brilliant star of Bethlehem,
*   How gracious are thy gleams!*
Yet countless souls of earthland
*   Know not thy saving beams.*
Apart from thee we journey,
*   Preferring dark to light—*
Desert us not, still shine for us,
*   And clear our darkened sight.*

"O little town of Bethlehem,
*   How still we see thee lie!*
Above thy deep and dreamless sleep
*   The silent stars go by":*
Rebuke us for our restlessness;
*   Bring peace again, we pray;*
Let justice reign, with mercy,
*   On this fair Christmas Day.*

—THOMAS CURTIS CLARK.

"What Christmas Means to Me"

"And the Word became flesh, and dwelt among us, and we beheld His glory, the glory as of the only begotten of the Father, full of grace and truth." (John 1:14.)

A Christmas Revery by P. O. BERSELL

Illustrated by Arthur Nelson

This reading, with organ accompaniment, was used by the author at a Christmas carol service. The melodies used for the musical accompaniment are indicated by the index numbers.

TODAY[1] I shall not even attempt to preach to you. Somehow Christmas Eve does not seem to be meant for preaching. That belongs to the Christmas Day itself, when the climax of the festival is reached in the temple worship of song and sermon in which are blended divine and human love and joy, and God speaks to us again with the proclamation of the fulfilment of prophecy—that a Child is born, a Son is given—the Prince of Peace, our Savior. Today, as we pause for a few moments amid the singing of the winsome and gladsome Christmas carols that somehow cause our hearts to throb in accord with the universal joy of all peoples of the earth, and with the refrains of the beloved Christmas hymns coming as gentle and soothing echoes of heaven to our souls, let us indulge in a little Christmas revery.

It[2] isn't mine alone. It isn't just for myself that I speak. I am trying to speak for you, to give utterance to the dreamings of your innermost soul, often vague and inarticulate, not always happy or beautiful, but on Christmas Eve they become clear and distinct, touched by the magic wand of an unseen hand, the inspiration which comes to you the night of the great mystery, when heaven touches earth. If I succeed in saying what you feel, and thus help you to appreciate more the beauty of this day and bring to a head the strange emotions that well up in your soul, so that this Christmas will mean more to you than just another Christmas, I will feel amply repaid.[3]

I PICTURE you in your home this Christmas Eve. It is night and the day's festivities are over. You have spent the evening with the family round about the tree. What a great night it has been! The eyes of old and young shone, not only with the reflected glint of the glittering tree, but with the brightness of an inward joy. Cheery voices joined in the singing of the old, old songs of praise to the Christ Child, and heads were bowed in reverence as the story of the first Christmas night was read. But even so the eyes of the little ones were turned with impatient anticipation and curiosity to the pile of packages around the foot of the tree, and when the brief devotions were over, there was a lusty chorus of: "Now we can open them!" And as they were distributed one by one, the opening of each one was accompanied by many an oh! and ah! of happy surprise.[4]

Now it's all over. The wrapping papers which covered the floor like heaped snowdrifts have been gathered and brought to the basement. The presents have been placed in neat piles, each to its owner. The family is in bed and all is quiet. You have attended to the last-minute duties of the household, and are ready to retire. You step into the living room where the lights of the tree are still burning. But before you turn them out, you sit down in the easy-chair. You relax comfortably and give yourself up to lonely musings, to hold converse with your soul, in Christmas revery.[5]

And this is what you say:

Oh, how tired I am! I didn't know that I was so tired. It's been a long hard pull to get ready for this day. But it's been worth it. I don't regret it. How happy everybody seemed to be! Love's labor was not lost. Every year, in the midst of my Christmas preparations, I have wished that there were no such things as all this Christmas work and worry. Now I'm sorry that I ever had such a thought. I'm tired, but I'm so deliciously tired.

MOST of our days are sort of drab. Our home is mostly a workshop, just doing the same things over and over again, long after they have ceased to be interesting. There isn't much poetry in the daily chores. And everybody gets impatient and dissatisfied.

It isn't so at Christmas. That brings a little bit of heaven into our home. It gives beauty to the commonplace things and makes everybody more loving and lovable.[6]

Look at all those gifts! We didn't have so much money to spend this year as usual and other people were pretty much in the same situation—and yet everybody was well remembered. The gifts I bought weren't so expensive. I saw so many things that I would rather have bought, but I don't think they would have brought greater joy to my loved ones. And I also received gifts, more than I expected. Best of all, I know that those who gave them to me love me. It makes me feel good to know that I'm appreciated, that there are those who really care for me and want me to be happy. I am happy tonight.[7]

There is that big pile of Christmas cards. They've come from all over the country. Some even have foreign stamps on them. Here's a card from some folks that we haven't sent a card to for years. They must really care for us and want our friendship. Thank God for friendship. It seems that it's just like scores of my friends coming to visit me tonight. Yes, some of them must have spent quite some time selecting just the card that would bring me the message of their heart. God bless them! I wonder if anybody right now is reading one of the cards I sent. Now, here's a beautiful card with a lovely sentiment. No, I can't take time to go over them all again tonight. I will do it tomorrow.[8]

MY home never looked so lovely before. I know it's the same old place. There's the old furniture that I have wanted to get rid of and buy one of the wonderful sets that they're selling at such a reasonable price now. I had hoped to do so this year. Somehow it all looks different tonight. Is it the tree that does it? I can just look at that tree and dream and dream. The tiny lights against the evergreen, like the loves and desires and joys of folks like myself against the background of God's promises. Now I know what it is. Christmas brings to me the reality of my life, which is my hope. For He has come who is to fulfill the desires of our heart. Only so can I make my home that which I want it to be, a nursery of the kingdom of heaven, where love rules supreme.[9]

Yes, it isn't much of a home, compared to what some people live in. But I thank God for its comfort, its protection, its love. Tonight it is more than a house. It's the palace of the King.

I'm so glad that we have kept up the old tradition of reading God's Word, the story of the birth of Jesus, before we distribute the gifts. Tonight I felt that it made a sacred place of our home. And I believe that even the children caught the spirit of it. At any rate they'll have some holy memories when they grow old, and they'll thank us for them.[10]

Memories! This is no time for tears but I just can't help it. There's a lump in my throat. I can see them, father and mother and my sisters and brothers, around the tree in my childhood home. It seems only yesterday, but it's longer than that. Father was a Christian man, a noble soul, and on Christmas Eve he read the Word of God like a priest in his own home, and the light of God was upon the face of dear old mother as she listened with folded hands. It's one of the bright spots in the hall of remembrance. Never again will we celebrate Christmas together on earth.

Oh, how many of our friends have passed on! Why is it that I think of them just now? Well, it's a good time to think of them. For Christmas tells me that friendship, in Jesus, is an everlasting friendship. We shall meet our friends again. And families that have learned to sing:[11]

> Come Jesus, glorious heavenly Guest,
> Keep Thine own Christmas in our breast,
> Then David's harp strings, hushed so long,
> Shall swell our jubilee of song—

such families shall be reunited in the everlasting Christmas.

NO, I can't sit here dreaming with my eyes open all night. I'll have to get to bed and sleep for a few hours so that I can get up for the early matins in church.[12] I wouldn't miss that beautiful service which has become dear to my heart. That's about as near to heaven as I ever expect to get here on earth. I want to be there to sing the songs our fathers and mothers sang:

> All hail to thee, O blessed morn!
> When unto earth, in glorious ray,
> Descends the gift of heaven!
> Singing, ringing
> Sounds are blending,
> Praises sending
> Unto heaven
> For the Savior to us given.

That's God's great gift to me. I can't give Him much in return.[13] I do not have gold, frankincense and myrrh, but it wouldn't be Christmas if I did not give Him something, as my Christmas gift, at least the price of a gift to one of my loved ones on earth. So I'm glad that I've been able to save out something for Him, who is my Savior, to help bring the glad tidings of salvation to all the world.

But I must go now. I'll have to turn out the light on the tree. There! How dark it is! But I'm not afraid of darkness—not of any darkness. For it's Christmas. God's angels are near, and

> . . . in the darkness shineth
> The everlasting light.[14]

MELODIES

[1]It Came Upon a Midnight Clear.
[2]Good News from Heaven the Angels Bring.
[3]Silent Night, Holy Night.
[4]Day Is Dying in the West.
[5]Love's Old Sweet Song.
[6]We Three Kings of Orient Are.
[7]Calm on the Listening Ear of Night.
[8]Tannenbaum.
[9]Home, Sweet Home.
[10]Auld Lang Syne.
[11]Chime, Happy Christmas Bells, Once More.
[12]All Hail to Thee, O Blessed Morn.
[13]O Little Town of Bethlehem.
[14]Joy to the World.

Christmas   Poetry

NO ROOM IN THE INN

No room for Him.
We grieve that it was so.
And then we go,
Busy upon our way,
With no more courtesy than they
Who turned our Lord away.

Our rooms are full,
There is so much to do,
Each day so new.
I wonder if the Lord of all
Is sad we grant Him space so small,
Less than a manger stall?

        —VIVYEN BREMNER.

Poems
Selected by
Thomas Curtis Clark

CAROL

Ah, dearest Jesus, holy Child,
Make Thee a bed, soft, undefiled,
Within my heart, that it may be
A quiet chamber kept for Thee.
My heart for very joy doth leap,
My lips no more can silence keep,
I too must sing, with joyful tongue,
That sweetest ancient cradle song,
"Glory to God in highest heaven,
Who unto man His Son hath given."
While angels sing, with pious mirth,
A glad New Year to all the earth.

        —MARTIN LUTHER.

Illustration
Madonna and Child
By Batoni

THE LORD OF THE WORLD

Come sail with me o'er the golden sea
To the land where the rainbow ends,
Where the rainbow ends,
And the great earth bends
To the weight of the starry sky,
Where the tempests die with a last fierce cry,

And never a wind is wild.
There's a mother mild, with a little Child
Like a star set on her knee;
Then bow you down, give Him the crown;
'Tis the Lord of the world you see.

        —G. A. STUDDERT-KENNEDY.

CHRISTMAS EVERYWHERE

Everywhere, everywhere, Christmas tonight!
Christmas in lands of the fir-tree and pine,
Christmas in lands of the palm-tree and vine,
Christmas where snow peaks stand solemn and white,
Christmas where corn fields stand sunny and bright.
Christmas where children are hopeful and gay,
Christmas where old men are patient and gray,
Christmas where peace, like a dove in his flight,
Broods o'er brave men in the thick of the fight;
Everywhere, everywhere, Christmas tonight!
For the Christ-Child who comes is the Master of all;
No palace too great, no cottage too small.

        —PHILLIPS BROOKS.

THE SHEPHERD SPEAKS

Out of the midnight sky a great dawn broke,
And a voice, singing, flooded us with song.
In David's city was He born, it sang,
A Savior, Christ the Lord. Then while I sat
Shivering with the thrill of that great cry,
A mighty choir, a thousand-fold more sweet,
Suddenly sang, Glory to God, and peace—
Peace on the earth; my heart, almost unnerved
By that swift loveliness, would hardly beat.
Speechless we waited till the accustomed night
Gave us no promise more of sweet surprise;
Then scrambling to our feet, without a word
We started through the fields to find the Child.

        —JOHN ERSKINE.

LIGHT AT CHRISTMAS

The centuries, since Christ to earthland came,
  Are all aflame
  With His fair fame.

The nations that have fallen in decay
  In sad tones say:
  "His is the way."

In this dark age of turpitude and blight,
  Out from the night
  Shines clear His light.

        —THOMAS CURTIS CLARK.

Christmas at Bethlehem, Jerusalem,

COME with me on a little trip to Bethlehem of Judea, where Jesus was born on the first Christmas Day. Christmas assumes a new meaning to one who has visited the birthplace of Jesus, the little town of Bethlehem, set high in the center of the Judean mountain range, with the Dead Sea and the mist-covered mountains of Moab lying in full view just to the east and stretching eastward from the little town and the Church of the Nativity, the spacious fields where on one memorable night, under a midnight sky, shepherds watched their flocks.

I saw shepherds watching their flocks on a summer's afternoon this year, and the sheep still know their master's voice and the shepherds still call the sheep by name. The shepherds of old, in their long, flowing white robes with a burnoose or a fez on their heads, may still be seen among the peasants of the East.

Down beneath the great stone basilica of the church which was built by Helena, mother of Constantine the Great, and is still standing in the nave of the Church of the Nativity, in a little chapel cut out of a limestone cliff, is the simple grotto cavern where, years ago, among the simple animals of the field, their bodies steaming after their day's work, and giving forth a natural heat to warm the chill of the stone cavern, a little Baby was born to Mary of Nazareth, a Baby who was destined to change the course of human history and become the world's supreme revelation of the character and workings of almighty God. Luke tells that a heavenly chorus filled the midnight sky with radiance and song: "Peace on earth, good-will toward men." By that angelic pæan of peace and good-will, nations, individuals, homes, and the great worlds of business and commerce, of states and nations, are still being judged and the future course of history will be charted toward a more brotherly and cooperative world, away from the chaos of former civilizations that became so greedy for their own gain and their selfish interests that they completely forgot the interests of others.

To me the mystery and wonder of Christmas Day are greatly multiplied when I see with my own eyes the tininess of Bethlehem and Judea, the simplicity and humility of those who first were permitted to witness the Incarnation, and how providentially and wondrously have come the great changes in human life and conduct that have issued from so small and simple a beginning.

So with us the small daily words and deeds of kindness and brotherliness that we utter or create may have an unexpected and marvelous consummation in the world in which we live, both present and future. The midnight song was heard by only a few simple men, intent on their duty, a hard

and on the Mount of Olives

O'FERRALL

and rigorous life, tending sheep committed to their charge, day and night throughout the year. So also to us as we fulfill the smallest and most arduous tasks may come great revelations. The simplicity and apparent smallness of the first Christmas should be an antidote against discouragement and despair, when we think of the narrow lot and the almost impossible difficulties that seem to face us in this human life.

COME with me also as we drive around the city walls of Jerusalem, across the Brook Kidron, to the Mount of Olives just beyond. Many gnarled old olive trees, which authorities tell us are well over eighteen hundred years old, still lift their rather gaunt branches toward the sky. Under them Jesus probably agonized and sweat drops of blood in the Garden of Gethsemane one memorable night. A few moments of meditation and of wrestling with your own temptations are quite in keeping with your thoughts as they race back to Christ in Gethsemane.

Upward a narrow road winds, and soon we reach the top of the Mount of Olives, where, in a reverent, hushed voice, our guide says, so simply: "From this spot our Savior ascended into heaven."

In our party was a man who was rather skeptical as to

religious beliefs, in fact you might almost call him an atheist. I recall how one day in Marseilles he was complaining rather bitterly about the amount of time that was spent in visiting cathedrals and churches. He reminded our guide several times that he had come to see the cities of the old world and to study the habits and customs of the people. I had wondered then how he would endure several days in the Holy Land, for there the religious memories would be paramount and all-absorbing in their interest.

In the Church of the Holy Sepulchre, as with lighted tapers we were descending into the dark cavern at whose end lay two stone crypts, the garden tomb of Joseph of Arimathea, where our Lord's body had lain before His resurrection, I noticed that the man was strangely silent, but I did not disturb his thoughts.

However, as we stood on the Ascension Mount and our guide reminded us of how, long ago, from that spot, as the Gospels tell us, our Lord disappeared from His apostles and they heard angelic voices saying: "Ye men of Galilee, why stand ye gazing up into heaven? This same Jesus, which is taken up from you to heaven, shall so come in like manner as ye have seen him go into heaven," I turned to our unbelieving friend and said: "All this must be intolerable to you—just so much fancy, legend, and tradition." To

19

CHRIST ON THE MOUNT
OF OLIVES

*A*ND *when he was come near, he beheld the city, and wept over it, Saying, If thou hadst known, even thou, at least in this thy day, the things which belong unto thy peace! but now they are hid from thine eyes. For the days shall come upon thee, that thine enemies shall cast a trench about thee, and compass thee round, and keep thee in on every side, And shall lay thee even with the ground, and thy children within thee; and they shall not leave in thee one stone upon another; because thou knewest not the time of thy visitation.*

—Luke 19:41-44.

Illustrated by R. J. Norman

my amazement he replied: "I am not in a mood to argue. I am almost willing to accept it all!"

I MET no one during our Holy Land stay who desired to argue. The sacred memories go far beyond mental processes, they penetrate to heart and soul. While the physical characteristics of Palestine today are cold and repellent most of the year—with fields, hills, and valleys absolutely devoid of grass, flowers, or trees—its very bleakness and ruggedness give a sense of spiritual power correspondingly keen and intense.

In endless, undulating, stony waves, purplish-brown in color, the hills lift themselves to the far horizon: gaunt, barren, soul-chilling. There are stones, thousands of them, everywhere—little wonder Jesus used them as symbols so often. Thousands of little black goats and white sheep pick their way up the stony hillsides, getting what little nourishment they can from tiny blades of grass among the rocks. How readily one understands why Jesus referred so frequently to sheep and goats.

Then the tininess of the Holy Land! From Mizpah or Nebo's height one can actually see it all. God's promise to Moses was literally true, as he gazed on the land he could

not enter. There lies snow-topped Mt. Hermon to the north, with the Jordan River winding its sinuous serpentine way through the waters of Merom and the Sea of Galilee, until it drops into the Dead Sea, thirteen hundred feet below sea level. To the east are the mist-covered hills of Moab, with the Dead Sea beneath, and to the west the fertile coastal plain, where Philistine cities, proud in their strength, mocked Saul and David long ago. Now these cities are only ruins, with the blue waters of the Mediterranean Sea beyond. To the south is the desert, and the picture is complete—in one panoramic sweep you can see it all!

The view from that spot is unforgettable. Behind us, bathed in the last warm rays of the setting sun, lay little Bethany, the home of Mary, Martha, and Lazarus, set like a jewel on her hilltop. Across the steep chasm of the Kidron lay the Holy City, surrounded in front of us by her walls. To the left steep above the gorge, lay the temple area, where now rises the magnificent Mosque of Omar, made of white stone and surmounted by its golden dome, where once rose, in proud glory, Herod the Great's gorgeous golden and white temple. This is the temple Jesus knew—of which He prophesied: "Not one stone shall remain upon another!"

Whatever outward changes the centuries have wrought as conquering armies succeeded one another in laying waste

CHRIST IN THE HOME OF
MARY AND MARTHA

NOW it came to pass, as they went, that he entered into a certain village: and a certain woman named Martha received him into her house. And she had a sister called Mary, which also sat at Jesus' feet, and heard his word. But Martha was cumbered about much serving, and came to him, and said, Lord, dost thou not care that my sister hath left me to serve alone? bid her therefore that she help me. And Jesus, answered and said unto her, Martha, Martha, thou art careful and troubled about many things: But one thing is needful: and Mary hath chosen that good part, which shall not be taken away from her.

—Luke 10:38-42.

Illustrated by R. J. Norman

and desolating the Holy City, the view we saw that early evening, of Zion on her holy mountain, must have been substantially the same that the Master saw when, coming one morning from the home of Mary and Martha in Bethany, He paused on the summit of Olivet and, seeing the city He loved wrapped in the lavish beauty of castles, theatres, palaces and the temple, which Herod the great builder had created there, and perceiving how proudly her political and religious leaders gloried in her material magnificence, while their inner lives decayed, He cried out in the anguish of His spirit: "O Jerusalem, Jerusalem, how often would I have gathered thee unto me, as a hen gathereth her chicks under her wings, but ye would not!"

THIS is the peculiar charm of the Mount of Olives: the view of the Holy City beyond Kidron. For the city, four-square on her Holy Mount, has risen again from her ashes and the Master's words have taken on a new significance, as the eternal spiritual destiny of Jerusalem flashes forth again in new beauty nearly two thousand years after the city Jesus knew was destroyed. You realize that Jerusalem is unconquerable and timeless, as are the messages of

One who trod those slopes as He gave the world its supreme conception of God and man!

Then, you remember that from this tiny, barren, hilly country, far away, came the world's highest moral and spiritual revelations. It is the birthplace of two religions—Judaism and Christianity—and the shrine of a third—Mohammedanism. Its very barrenness and ruggedness speak of God and great spiritual truths. How often life's richest treasures come from its most forbidding aspects! For Palestine and Jerusalem are eternal! Their invisible contribution to life's progress can never be measured with man's measuring line! As you traverse Bethlehem's fields and Olivet's slopes, these thoughts fill your mind, so appropriately expressed in William Blake's lines:

> Bring me my bow of burning gold,
> Bring me my arrows of desire!
> Bring me my spear! O clouds unfold!
> Bring me my chariot of fire!
> I will not cease from mental fight:
> Nor shall my sword sleep in my hand
> Till I have built Jerusalem
> In all God's green and pleasant land.

Christmas   Poetry

THE CHRISTMAS STAR

High in the heavens a single star,
  Of pure, imperishable light;
Out on the desert strange and far
  Dim riders riding through the night:
Above a hilltop sudden song
  Like silver trumpets down the sky—
And all to welcome One so young
  He scarce could lift a cry!

Stars rise and set, that star shines on:
  Songs fail, but still that music beats
Through all the ages come and gone,
  In lane and field and city streets.
And we who catch the Christmas gleam,
  Watching with children on the hill,
We know, we know it is no dream—
  He stands among us still!

  —NANCY BYRD TURNER.

MADONNA AND CHILD
by Barocci

Poems
Selected by
Thomas Curtis Clark

THE LIGHT OF BETHLEHEM

'Tis Christmas night! The snow,
  A flock unnumbered, lies:
The old Judean stars, aglow,
  Keep watch within the skies.

An icy stillness holds
  The pulses of the night:
A deeper mystery infolds
  The wondering hosts of light.

Till, lo, with reverence pale
  That dims each diadem,
The lordliest, earthward bending, hail
  The light of Bethlehem!

  —JOHN B. TABB.

A CHRISTMAS PRAYER

We open here our treasures and our gifts;
And some of it is gold,
And some is frankincense,
And some is myrrh;
For some has come from plenty,

Some from joy,
And some from deepest sorrow of the soul.
But Thou, O God, dost know the gift is love,
Our pledge of peace, our promise of good-will.
Accept the gift and all the life we bring.

  —HERBERT H. HINES.

MAGI—OF OLD AND TODAY

Away from the palace of comfort and ease,
  Over mountain and desert afar,
Till down to the lowliest stable it led,
  They followed the gleam of His star.

Away from the mansions of selfish desire,
  To hovels of want and despair,
The star of the Christ is still leading the way,
  That man may discover Him there.

  —HERBERT J. DORAN.

A CHRISTMAS CAROL

There's a song in the air!
There's a star in the sky!
There's a mother's deep prayer
And a baby's low cry!
And the star rains its fire while the Beautiful sing,
For the manger of Bethlehem cradles a King.

There's a tumult of joy
O'er the wonderful birth,
For the virgin's sweet boy
Is the Lord of the earth,
Ay! the star rains its fire and the Beautiful sing,
For the manger of Bethlehem cradles a King.

In the light of that star
Lie the ages impearled;
And the song from afar
Has swept over the world.
Every hearth is aflame and the Beautiful sing
In the homes of the nations that Jesus is King.

We rejoice in the light,
And we echo the song
That comes down through the night
From the heavenly throng.
Ay! we shout to the lovely evangel they bring,
And we greet in His cradle our Savior and King!

  —JOSIAH GILBERT HOLLAND.

Christmas in America

By JOHN T. FARIS

THE love of holidays and feasting was brought to the Colonies by the first emigrants to the new land—that is, unless they were Puritans or Quakers. The Puritans of New England for many years denied the Christmas festival to their children as well as to their elders. Governor Bradford in 1621 said that a Christmas celebration could not be tolerated; it was a relic of popery. Even as late as 1657 the General Court of Massachusetts provided a penalty of five shillings for each one who failed to regard the law which forbade the observance of "any such day as Christmas or the like, either by forbearing of labor, feasting, or in any other way." Though this law was repealed in 1681, the feeling against the day persisted.

Yet now what a glorious festival Christmas is in the New England homes! How the doors are opened wide to members of the family, long absent, as they come under the old roof-tree to feast, to give, to worship Him of whom New England's loved poet, Longfellow, wrote:

> Then pealed the bells more loud and deep;
> God is not dead; nor doth He sleep!
> The wrong shall fail,
> The right prevail,
> With peace on earth, good-will to men!

SINCE the twelfth century the English have gloried in their Christmas season, their feasting, their home merriment, their singing of carols, and, above all, the joy that comes through sharing with others, both in the home and out of the home, the gladness of the Christmastide, when on every side are heard the echoes of the prayer:

> God bless you, merry gentlemen!
> May nothing you dismay!

This festival of holly, mistletoe, red berries, ivy, turkeys, geese, game, poultry, brawn, meat, pigs, sausage, oysters, pie, puddings, fruit; this season, when the tree is loaded with gifts and the homes full of eager youth and gratified older people, has been transplanted from England to Canada, where hearts are the same from the St. Lawrence to the Yukon and from Labrador to British Columbia, where the question asked in other countries, "Shall we have snow for Christmas?" gives way to the query, "How much snow shall we have?"

There is Christmas weather everywhere: and everywhere Christmas makes glad the hearts of men and women and children, whether they live in comfortable farm houses, in villages, by the lakes, or in bustling cities. In the hearts of all alike resounds the glad message:

> Oh, that birth for ever blessed!
> When the Virgin, full of grace,
> By the Holy Ghost conceiving,
> Bore the Savior of our race,
> And the Babe, the world's Redeemer,
> First revealed His sacred face
> Evermore and evermore.

(From Prudentius: Of the Father's Son Begotten)

THERE are misguided people who say that a country without hills or mountains has no claim to beauty. What of Indiana, then? And what of the traveler who declared just such a country as Indiana to be "the most beautiful country upon the face of the earth"? In summer, when the wind blows in the trees, when the corn rises ten feet high in the rich fields, and the wheat is like the billows of the sea, that is the region to which the hearts of many turn with longing. And in winter! How glorious the same trees are when snow and sleet cover them with white beauty! How the snow crystals in the ice glisten in the sunshine! Shadows cast on the snow by the bare branches seem like bridges for the crossing of fancy. Yonder in the cornfield shocks of corn are wearing so jauntily their crowns of white. Just beyond is a field where the snow has made of unsightly gullies bits of beauty, by reason of the mantle winter has thrown over them!

Have you ever on Christmas Eve crossed such fields in a sled, when fences were laid aside for the passage, making the journey to the little church much easier? What a preparation is such a passage, over snow glistening in the December moonlight, for joining with gladness in the song by the community Christmas tree:

The winter night was dark and still,
    The village lay asleep;
In meadows underneath the hill
    The shepherds watched their sheep:
The shepherds watched their sheep, good Lord,
    But angels watched o'er Thee,
While Mary held Thee to her heart,
    And they sang jubilee.

(From "A Carol for Christmas Eve," by Louis F. Benson)

ALONG watercourses like the Brandy-wine, the Juniata, and the Kiskimi-netas, Pennsylvania pioneers built their mills for grinding grain. Here and there pictur-esque survivals of other days tell of the ac-tivities of those pioneers; often the old mills are still doing their service, and stones are grinding exceedingly fine.

Fortunately, too, there are survivals in the old Keystone state of the men of faith who ran these mills, many of whom heard God speaking to them in the spring when the waters were plentiful, and again at the Christmas season, when winter put its stern clasp of ice on creeks and rivers.

Can't you picture the old miller standing by the ice-bound stream, bowing his head by the side of the channels of brooks that pass away, which are black by reason of the ice?

But winter, with all its beauty, could not be a time of rejoicing if it were not for the knowledge that He who has sent the ice and the snow will also, in the appointed time, send the warm sun that will loosen the bonds of the ice, melt the river, and make the earth take on the glory of spring, the beauty of summer!

So in the midst of winter's snow and ice we worship God, the Savior, who came to earth on that Christmas morn when shep-herds, following the guiding star, found the Babe lying in a manger. The Savior has shown us how we and all people everywhere may be transformed into usefulness and beauty, even as the snow and ice give way to the warm beauty of spring and summer.

To Him we pray at the Christmas season, and always:

Lord Jesus, look on me,
    And purge away my sin.
From earth-born passion set me free,
    And make me pure within.

COLORADO offers an impressive setting for Christmas: Mountains pointing to Him who created a beautiful world that we might enjoy it—mountains like the Sangre de Cristo range, which led Bayard Taylor to exclaim: "In variety, in harmony of form, in effect against the dark blue sky, in breadth and grandeur, I know no picture of the Alps which can be placed beside it!" What supreme mountain majesty! Glorious parks lie hidden amid towering heights—parks where mighty forests contrast their living green with the eternal snows on the peaks that rise above them! Is there anything like the vision of Long's Peak and its neighbors from Rocky Mountain Park, or of the Sangre de Cristo range from the San Isabel National Forest, where one hundred miles of supreme mountain majesty awe the beholder, as they rise, like soldiers in a row or like the work of engineers who have designed a perfect succession of monumental structures?

But what engineer could have planned such perfection? There is but One. No wonder the Spanish explorer who saw them while the setting sun crowned the snowclad heights with glory, exclaimed, "Sangre de Cristo! Blood of Christ!" or that he was unhappy until he came to what seemed to be the miraculous white cross on the mountain he named "The Mount of the Holy Cross."

Colorado's heights speak eloquently of Him to whom we are invited to lift our eyes, and its snows tell of the purity He gives to those who seek atonement through the blood of Christ, who was born at Bethlehem, whose praises we sing at Christmastide, and in whose strength we may live throughout the year, until the joy of Christmas permeates all of life.

Colorado is indeed a Christmas land.

THOUGH it may seem improper to choose the name Paradise for any earthly location, there seems to be justification for it in the case of Paradise Valley on Mount Rainier, Washington's glorious monument. For Paradise Valley, a vision of beauty and glory, bursts on the climber who has spent several hours toiling upward. And what a vision such a climb affords! By an easy grade the way leads through forests, along canyons, by the Nisqually, with its brief tumultuous course from the glacier to the sea, up to the very gates of Mount Rainier National Park. Then across winding streams, above the tops of lofty trees, through canyons surmounted by engineering triumphs, within sight of leaping waterfalls, to the bridge that crosses the Nisqually only a few hundred feet below the spot where the waters flow from under the ice of the parent glacier. Finally comes the steep climb to Paradise Valley, the abode of flowers in summer, the scene of great ski contests in winter, the point from which majestic views may be secured at all seasons.

There those who feel that they must have snow and ice for their Christmas may go from the smiling valleys where sunshine and rain alternate more or less pleasantly throughout the winter months. And what a Christmas setting: mighty evergreens banked with snow until they are like great white statues, and snow piled high along the trail and on the roofs of every building! Many choose to combine the white beauty of Paradise Valley with the home Christmas tree, lighted in memory of the star of Bethlehem, laden with gifts expressive of love for Him to whom the Wise Men brought gold, frankincense, and myrrh.

AS the Babe born at Bethlehem more than nineteen hundred years ago grew through boyhood to young manhood, He became familiar with a land beautiful and fertile—for in that day Palestine was really "a land flowing with milk and honey." In many ways it resembled California. There were mountains and luxuriant trees. There were vineyards and orchards; figs and olives grew in profusion. Flowers were everywhere. Jesus delighted in all these things. How intimately He knew them! In later years He was able to draw vivid lessons from wild flowers, birds, trees, vineyards, fields of grain.

California, then, should be a help in interpreting the Bible, in making real the life of the Son of God, who came to earth for our salvation. This is especially true at Christmas. Yonder, to the east, is the desert, similar to the country over which the Wise Men traveled to bring their gifts; nearer at hand are pastures, like those where shepherds watched their sheep by night. And everywhere are the people for whom Jesus chose to be born a man, subject to the limitations, the difficulties, the anxieties of life on earth.

IN that land of dazzling contrasts, varying from the sparkling waters of Carlsbad Cavern to Capulin Mountain, from the mysterious Stone Lions of the Rito de los Frijoles to the canyons in whose walls peoples of long ago had their homes of wonder, Christmas has been a festival of moment since the first Spanish explorers came up from old Mexico and told the Indians of the Christ Child, whose birth then is celebrated. In 1540 the priests with Coronado brought to the squat adobe house of Isleta — approached by outside ladders, with ceiling beams projecting from the walls—the story that was told in Judean homes nineteen hundred years ago. And in some of the very homes that stood there on the lofty plateau missionaries today are repeating the same story of the Savior who was born at Bethlehem.

Here and there, close to these simple folk, live also English-speaking people who have planted their homes in this country of rare air and bright sunshine. They, too, find delight at Christmas time in festivals, in gifts, in songs. They do not need to send to Maine or Michigan for Christmas trees, for these grow, of rare beauty, of infinite variety, in their own land.

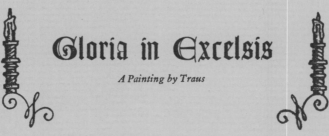

Gloria in Excelsis

A Painting by Traus

Ye Olde Merrie Yuletide of England

By CLARENCE B. LUND

ENGLAND is often referred to as the "land of merrie Christmas." It surely knows how to make happiness contagious. The happiest people are those at the inns. Here the long flames from the burning yule log cast their streaky shadows across the open room. People coming and going shout their greetings. The inn-keeper looks like a rosy apple as he wabbles back and forth, making things ready.

As the meal is being prepared, there is an odor of plum pudding and delicious vegetables. As the guests take their seats, they are anxious and flush with anticipation. The great feast is about to begin. The fellowship is high, hearts are light and happy. Neighbor greets neighbor and all seem truly to be at peace with one another. The poor man from across the way has been invited. The widow with her baby is asked to join. The sailor from the coast, who has weathered many a port, is asked to share the bounties of the well filled table. The carolers on their way about the neighborhood are asked to join the party.

Suddenly the door opens. Ah, here comes the inn-keeper. But much as the guests love the old inn-keeper, something else has their attention. He is carrying on a platter, richly garnished, the *head of a boar!*

As the procession enters with all the goodies, the fiddler starts playing and the villagers join in an old song, long wrapped in English tradition: "To the Boar's Head." Students, mothers, fathers, and all other villagers know the song and sing it heartily in the old Latin.

Thus has begun Ye Olde Merrie Yuletide of England. At its root, it is deeply religious, on the surface, just a merrie time.

The Happy Christmas Comes Once More

By CLARENCE B. LUND

A GREAT hush settles upon the land at the twilight hour as the bells in a thousand towers begin to ring in Christmas in Norway.

The Cathedral at Trondheim, the finest sanctuary in the whole country, the pride of the people, a little while ago stood sharply etched against the darkening sky. Now the slowly and silently falling snow almost obscures it from sight. A soft light streams through the colored windows and touches the falling snow flakes with an almost unearthly beauty.

And all the time the bells chime in the tall tower, calling old and young to Vesper Service.

From different parts of the city people wend their way to the beloved sanctuary. They come singly, by twos and threes; slowly, reverently; listening to the bells; looking at the falling flakes. Dear Christmas Eve!

As they enter the Cathedral they hear the soft, sweet tones of the organ; they see the lighted candles on the altar, revealing its pure whiteness. They enter the pews, bow their heads in prayer.

In one of the rear pews sits an elderly, gray-haired woman in silent prayer. Life has been hard on her. But all is now forgotten. God is good and life is sweet. Then memories of by-gone days flood her soul. She is a child again in the home up in the mountains. She is sitting in her mother's lap near the hearth stone as the flames throw a soft, quivering light on the nearest objects. As the choir begins to sing an old Christmas carol, her mother seems to join in with her sweet voice. She hears the choir no more, only mother. And this is the hymn she sings:

The Sleeping Child

By CLARENCE B. LUND

MARTIN LUTHER was a mighty man; so powerfully did he preach that he shook all Europe. Pope and prelates, emperor and princes, tried to put a stop to his preaching and writing, but of no avail. He feared God, but feared no man.

Luther was not only a great preacher through the spoken and written word, he was also a musician and a hymn writer. One of his hymns has been translated into more languages than any other hymn in the world. He also composed a melody to it. The more voices which join in singing it, the better it sounds. When sung by thousands of men and women, "A Mighty Fortress Is Our God" makes a powerful impression. It sounds like a battle cry on the day of victory.

But this strong and sturdy man, this "Oak of Saxony," was not only a fearless crusader and a singer of great hymns; he was a lover of children. His letter to one of his little sons is matchless in tenderness, humor and simplicity. He wrote songs for the children, too, and some of them are now sung by children in all lands.

Late one afternoon, while his wife is busy preparing for Christmas, Luther is sitting reading. The baby in the cradle begins to cry and the mother hastens to the cradle. She makes a sign with her hand to her husband. He understands and steps over to the cradle, sits down and begins to rock it gently. The baby soon falls asleep. With great tenderness Luther looks at the sleeping child. Ah, thus the Christ Child must have slept in the manger! It was probably on such an occasion that these beautiful lines came to his mind:

The Story of a Little French Girl

By CLARENCE B. LUND

A LITTLE French girl is trudging timidly from door to door one Christmas Eve. She is carrying a basket of cakes, which she is trying to sell. Her hands and feet are almost numb from cold, but she cannot go home before all the cakes are sold. Only then will there be Christmas dinner for her little brothers and sisters on the morrow.

Softly she raps on the door of a fine house. A kindly lady opens the door. "No, thank you, we have cakes," she says. The little girl makes several more unsuccessful attempts, then finally she sinks exhausted on the steps of a hovel. Soon she is asleep.

What a wonderful light surrounds her! There on a hill she sees shepherds who are looking up into the sky. She, too, looks up, and beholds a host of shining angels. Listen! They are singing a beautiful song. Suddenly, someone touches her arm gently, and she looks up into the kind face of a gentleman. "I'll buy your cakes," he says, handing her some money.

She runs home, her hands and feet no longer numb. All out of breath she rushes into the house, where mother, sisters, and brothers surround her and listen to her story.

"Can you sing the song the angels sang?" asks the mother. "No, but I'll sing you another song," and she sings the song which all French people sing on Christmas Eve:

The Star Over Byzantium

A Story of the Fourth Crusade

By WILLIAM H. LEACH

Illustrated by David Workman

PHILIP, squire to Louis de Chartes, noble baron of France, sat in his tent listening to the fall of the heavy rain. He had hoped that the stars would shine on Christmas Eve but there was little indication of it at present. Philip was far from his native France. Three years had passed since he kissed his father and mother and set out as squire in the conquest of the Holy Land. Three years, and still the French army and its Venetian allies were far from the Holy City.

Had the night been clear he could have seen from his tent the quiet waters of the Bosporus. On the south lay the queen city of the East, Byzantium, soon to be known as Constantinople. During the hours of the day he could look over the walls and see the domes and spires of its churches and public buildings. His liege lord, Louis, was even now in the city, meeting in a council of war. Philip had been left to protect his property.

LOUIS had been gone for some days. Momentous plans took time. Philip hoped fervently that there would be a decision to move on toward their original destination. He was tired of delay. The growing ill feeling among the various divisions of troops worried him. He wanted to save the Holy City and then go back to his native France.

Then he was worried about the boy Theodore. It was a strange thing which had brought the Greek boy into the tent of Louis. Philip had hoped that tonight the boy could go back to the city. It would create a difficult situation should the baron return and find the sick Greek lad in his bed. But it was Christmas Eve. One must deal with a guest in a spirit of kindness. One could not turn a stranger from a bed on Christmas Eve. If the stars would but shine it would be easy. But now Theodore, weakened by illness, was hardly in a fit condition to venture out.

Philip thought of his own home. He knew the hospitality which would be offered during the Christmas season. The sky over Byzantium, he meditated, was the same sky that covered Jerusalem and Bethlehem. Perhaps the star of Bethlehem had been so bright that if one had really looked he might have seen it from the plains of Byzantium.

PHILIP turned over in his mind all that had happened since he pledged himself to the holy cause. The day of his vow lived before him. It was in the parish church. With many others he had crowded to hear the priest read a letter from Pope Innocent III. It was a call for a new crusade. The full-toned voice of the priest made each word distinct:

"Arise, ye faithful; Arise, gird on the sword and buckler; Arise, hasten to the help of Jesus Christ; He Himself will lead your banner to victory."

The priest described conditions in the Holy Land. There had been crusades but the holy sepulchre was still in the hands of the Mohammedans. Christians had to pay a tax to see the birthplace of their Lord. The time had come for a new effort. Those who would offer their services were promised victory.

Philip remembered that tears came to the eyes of the strong men as the appeal was read and that they crowded to the altar to receive the blessing of the priest. When Louis de Chartes moved forward the boy Philip followed him. He kneeled at the left foot of his lord. When the assembly arose Louis saw him. He placed his hand on the boy's shoulder.

"No longer art thou apprentice, Philip," he said, "but now squire and knight to be."

PREPARATIONS for crusades are not accomplished overnight. Richard the Lion-Hearted had spent thirty of the best years of his life in the second crusade. Many of those who had gone away with him made their permanent homes in the East. Those who ventured on this new effort might expect years to pass before their return.

Lands and estates were sold and converted into gold. Gold, in the thirteenth century, as now, was the password to all parts of the earth. Many who could not themselves go brought their wealth to the churches and had it turned over to the sacred cause.

Transportation was a serious thing. Experience had shown that the advance should be made by sea. France possessed few ships. So it went to a neighbor, Venice, whose ships covered the earth. Louis had been one of the nobles selected to visit Venice and petition that nation for its cooperation and aid.

In the thirteenth century Venice was a mighty nation, one of the show places of the world. The Lion of St. Mark had been carried to every land. Every boat, on its return voyage from the East, brought back gold and silver, metal and wood to decorate its public buildings. So in the West one could feel the atmosphere of the East. There were columns, inlaid tiling, bronzes, and other valuable items. It was in the year 1201 A. D. that Philip first saw the Church of St. Mark. Of course, the famous bronze horses were not there. They were brought back later as trophies of this crusade.

THE nobles of France presented their request to the Council of Venice. They asked for transportation to Cairo for 4,500 knights, 9,000 squires, and 20,000 infantry. Philip, with others, crowded into the chamber as the council deliberated. French retainers mingled with Venetian merchants and artisans. Geoffroi Villehardouin, a friend of Louis de Chartes, was the spokesman for the French.

"Messieurs," he cried, "the noblest and most powerful barons of France have sent us to pray you to take pity on Jerusalem, in bondage to the Turk, and to crave that for God's love ye aid us to avenge the shame of Jesus Christ, for they know that no other nation is so mighty on the sea as yours; and therefore they have charged us to kneel before you till ye have granted their power and had pity on the Holy Land."

The populace waited with bated breath. The French nobles kneeled as if in prayer. The aged and blind Dandola was the doge of Venice. After consulting the council he arose and stretched forth his arms. In a loud voice he cried, "We grant it." The people took up the cry. Artisan embraced soldier. The pact was signed. Venice and France were allies in a holy war.

THEN followed the movement of the troops. It takes time to build and equip ships. So it was not until in October, 1202, that the sailing began. The blind Dandola was the leader. Troops, grown weary of waiting, took on new life now that the movement had actually begun.

But their joy was short-lived. A stop was made for the assault of Zara; then a second stop was made at Corfu. At a conference held here it was decided that the expedition should be deflected from its course long enough to conquer Constantinople and restore Emperor Alexius to his throne.

It was mid-summer of 1203 when the French had their first view of the queen city. They were moved by both admiration and terror. A historian relates that when they saw the length and breadth of the city which was the queen of all cities, there was none so bold but that his flesh crept with fear. These emotions possessed them when on a fine July morning the order to attack was given.

It was a battle which made history. Constantinople was well walled and fortified. The French made their attacks by land, although they knew little about this kind of assault. The Venetians attacked from their boats. The prows were guided up close to the walls, extension ladders were pushed over the walls, and soon fighters were landed in the city. Byzantium yielded and Alexius regained the throne.

NOW," thought Philip, "we shall move quickly on Jerusalem." But instead the army was detained in the wonderful city. The leaders held extended conferences with Emperor Alexius. Soldiers wandered through the streets. Those who were not motivated by religious sentiments were very much in sympathy with the idea of remaining here and enjoying the wealth the city offered.

It is not to be wondered at. The stores which crowded the narrow streets bulged with riches. There were gold and silver fittings, carpets and tapestries, leather and wooden carvings. It was a fairy city to these rough men from the West.

Here in the Hippodrome Square Philip had his first view of the famous bronze horses, which were among the priceless possessions of Byzantium. The admiring Westerners were informed that these horses first decorated the public buildings of Alexandria. Augustus Caesar brought them to Rome. Constantine took them from Rome to grace his new Eastern capitol. Shrewd Venetians stroked their beards and knowingly observed to one another: "They must go to Venice."

All the world now knows that they were carried to Venice. For generations they have added charm to that island city. Twice in time of war they have been removed to other lands for safe-keeping. But today, located in the piazzetta of Venice, they are perhaps the most treasured statuary in the world.

In the midst of such wealth cupidity took possession of the troops. Despite efforts by the leaders to check the practice, marauding expeditions made up of French and Venetian soldiers were constantly despoiling the Greeks of their possessions.

ONE night when Philip and a boy friend were wandering through the streets they saw some French troops fighting Greek merchants. The soldiers were evidently attempting to help themselves to some of the things they desired and the merchants were trying to protect their belongings. Among the fighters was a youth. He attacked the soldiers with vigor, but was struck down with a sword. Before further damage was done, however, the noise of mounted guards put the soldiers to rout.

Philip and his friend, Henry, succeeded in dragging the boy to the side of the road before the guards galloped by. Together they carried him to the tent of Louis, bathed him, and applied sweet oil to his wounds. As Louis was in the city, the boy was placed in the noble's bed.

"I feel that Sir Louis will not thank you for defiling his bed with a Greek," observed Henry.

"Louis is my liege lord," said Philip, "but I follow another, even Jesus Christ. He would say, 'If thine enemy hunger, feed him.' "

THE boy had not been seriously injured but he could not be moved for some days. Louis would probably be back at Christmas. By that time the youth should be able to return to his home.

As he grew stronger the two boys learned to know one another. Theodore was the name of the Greek. His father was a merchant. He had a brother and two sisters. His mother was living.

The attack of the French and Venetians had puzzled him.

"We are all followers of the Lord Jesus," he said. "Why do we fight one another?"

"I, too," said Philip, "have wondered about that. I pledged myself to fight the Turk, not the Greek."

"I must get home for the Lord's birthday," said Theodore. "It is always a wonderful time for us. In our churches there will be little mangers with angels over them. The choirs will sing their best. We will go into the churches and place little cakes and gifts for the Christ child. I could not think of being away on the Lord's birthday."

BUT the day before Christmas, even as preparations for the celebration were taking place, the great storm arose. It beat down in fury upon the tents. The soldiers, busy with their plans, considered it an ill omen.

"It is the Greek in Louis' tent," they said. "Our Lord is not pleased."

"I think we should go and see the squire, Philip, and insist that he put the Greek out," suggested one. Upon this they agreed.

Within the seclusion of the tent Theodore and Philip were talking things over.

"If the rain subsides I shall let you go," said Philip. "Here is a blanket for protection against the rain. Here is oil for your wounds. Now lie down and sleep. As soon as the storm abates I shall waken you."

THE Greek boy was soon asleep, deaf to the sound of murmuring voices which drew near. Philip, however, was conscious of them. And he knew the purpose. For his friend Henry had told him of the murmurings in the army against Theodore. When the voices shouted his name he opened the tent. (Concluded on page 58)

Till the Backlog Burns in Two

HE HAS HIS HARD TIMES, BUT THE SOUTHERN
NEGRO HAS HIS "BIG INNING" AT CHRISTMAS

By EDWIN B. CHAPPELL, JR.

Illustrated by R. and L. Koelnau

THERE was an honored tradition on the old southern plantation that until the Christmas backlog burned in two (it was rolled up by the strongest huskies on the place bright and early Christmas morning), the Negroes were free to indulge in as much frivolity as they might desire.

For nearly twelve months they conducted themselves in a manner befitting their station in the company of their "white folks," but when the Christmas backlog began to shoot forth its brilliant sparks, they had a new status. The "master" would smile at antics that only a few days earlier, or later, would have brought forth a storm of abuse. Darky voices, melodious and rich, that in normal times were raised only in the seclusion of dingy cabins, would burst forth in the most unexpected places.

Now the old South is only a thing of memory. The plantation, and all the gay life that went with it, is something that grandmother relates to her grandchildren—when they have time to listen!

"CHRISTMAS is such a calm season now," said a dear old lady the other day. She had passed her youth on a plantation in Mississippi, one hundred miles south of Memphis. "You should have been with us at Christmas in 1875. All the children had been off to boarding school and preparations had been made for our return weeks in advance. We brought cousins and friends with us without wondering whether or not there would be enough to eat, or whether we would make the burden too great for mother to bear. Didn't we know that the meat houses were filled with the finest meats? That there were sufficient turkeys on the place to feed a regiment? And that good old Lucinda and her able assistants could cook food for thirty as easily as for ten?

"The darkies—one hundred and fifty of them on the place —were all smiles. How good they looked to us as we rode our horses over the plantation! They were more thrilled over the thought of the little present that my father—who made the rounds on horseback with two huge sacks filled to the brim slung over the animal's back—was going to bring them than some modern children I know are over a whole room stuffed with expensive nothings.

"Such laughter! Such merriment! Everyone a king or a queen, from the tiniest pickaninny to our genial master— father himself! The meals we served would make the feasts of today appear like pink teas. There were entertainments put on by the talented darkies on our place, long horseback rides under the mild winter skies. One must have passed through it to understand the happiness, the good-will that seemed to permeate everything."

Let us shed a silent tear for the days that were. Distance, in time or miles, does lend enchantment.

BUT as far as the darkies are concerned, there is still something left of the Christmas of 1875, about which the old ladies of today delight to converse. It is a strange something that people from other sections find it difficult to understand.

In the first place, the treatment meted out to the Negro by the southern white man is a queer paradox. In the South we often hear something like this: "The white people of the South love the Negro as an individual, and look down upon him as a group, while in the North they look down upon him as an individual and love him as a group." Whether or not there is any truth in the latter part of this assertion, it can be said that the first part is based on some measure of fact.

The southern white man, especially the white man of the better class, has a feeling for the Negro individual that is closely akin to the feeling of a rich and kindly bachelor uncle for his nephews and nieces. Especially if the individual has worked for him, even though for a short period, does he feel that the man is his special ward. He must come to his assistance when hunger or sickness is present. He must use his influence to protect him when one of the natural enemies of the Negro—the loan shark and the deputy sheriff—gets too close on his heels. He may growl and threaten and use all manner of vile language, but the Negro holds his ground, cap in hand and eyes downcast, for he knows that sooner or later his "white folks" won't fail him.

The same white man who will shrug his shoulders and mumble something about "keeping the Negro in his place" when he reads of a lynching, or who will use his influence to keep the Negro in separate sections of the street car and in segregated districts of the community, or insist that the Negro do nothing that may give the slightest impression that he considers himself in any way the equal of his white brother—this same man will deny himself and his family in order to pay the police fine of Black Tom, on whom he has not laid eyes for five years.

The same man who will openly be a party to a scheme of things that makes it next to impossible for an intelligent Negro to find an opening of importance in the affairs of the South, will also confess that he feels lonesome when he does not have at least one or two Negroes working on his place.

UNLESS he is moved by the mob spirit, the southern white man simply cannot endure the sight of suffering in the case of any Negro who makes a personal appearance before him. He may know that only a few blocks away there lives a great crowd of black people without opportunity and without some of the things which he considers the necessities of life. And his knowledge will not move him to action. It is only when Amos or Lucy makes the appeal in person that his heart strings and purse strings are touched.

So it is that the Negro in the South with "white connections" is never forgotten at Christmas time. The servants in the home are as much a part of the Christmas celebration as the tree, or the turkey, or the plum pudding. Those who feel that they have any reason to believe they are favored "members" of the family will pay a visit a few days before Christmas to inform the head of the house that "you can look for me bright and early Christmas mornin'."

THE gifts have been piled high around the big tree in the den that has been a secret abode for several days. Boys and girls are scampering here and there, begging mother to hurry. Grown folks are tying up last-minute bundles. Father is dusting off his spectacles so that he can read the inscriptions without difficulty.

And off in the kitchen, Eliza, Tom and their children are waiting. They know that before long the call will come to them, just as it does to the children of the home. They know that under the tree are presents for every one of them.

Now comes the call. "Christmas gift!" rings through the house a hundred times. Darkies come pouring in from the kitchen. Kiddies are tumbling over each other in excitement. One of the older girls sits at the piano and plays, "O Little Town of Bethlehem."

Chairs have been provided for all. This is no time to think of "keeping the Negro in his place." His place is now with the other members of the family.

Father walks to the table. (What makes him so slow!) Jimmie, the youngest of the family, has been appointed messenger; his honored position is just at the side of father.

"For Mother—from Jimmie," father says finally, and mother exclaims as if she knew nothing about it.

"For Margaret—from her Dad," he announces a second time.

"For Eliza and Tom—from all the children."

Jimmie is kept busy. He hardly knows whether to dash back for another gift or to watch the expressions on the faces of the recipients as they open their packages. It is all such fun.

ESPECIALLY is it fun to watch old Tom, Eliza and the children. They are getting the things they have dreamed about, the things their own limited income would never permit. Their excited little cries of joy seem at times to drown out all the other noise. In their eyes a new light is shining, a light of childlike enthusiasm

Some would call it pathetic to watch them hurry off to the kitchen after the festivities are completed, their arms loaded with gaily colored packages. They would see in this little ceremony nothing more than the disheartening struggle of the Negro for a place in the white man's world. They would call attention to the fact that the Negro will never climb to great heights as long as he accepts his position as the white man's underling in this docile fashion.

But I wonder if out of the spirit of this season of seasons, that means so much to the Negro servant and helper of the South, will not come a new understanding and a new appreciation of the worth of a soul, be it black or white.

Progress, especially when it is running against the hard wind of prejudice, moves slowly. The Negro in the South, in spite of the fact that some of his own leaders and his own friends among the white race consider his present plight nothing short of deplorable, has gone far in the last fifty years. This journey upward has not come in jerks; it has been slow and steady.

Out of the mass of injustice and misunderstanding and brutality that forges to the front all too often, comes a small hand of fellowship and good-will that is raised toward the Negro these days in the South. The hand seems to be saying,

"I am going to do all in my power to pull you upward just a little higher than you have ever been before."

Generally, it is the hand of youth, the hand that has not been soiled by the contamination of prejudice.

ONLY recently a teen-age girl heard her mother complaining because two Negro women had been invited to attend her missionary meeting, where they had "occupied seats right next to ours."

"But Mother," said the girl, "why did you object to that? Was it because they were ignorant or dirty?"

"No, they were both intelligent and clean," replied her mother.

"Then I can't understand what you mean!" was this young girl's answer to her startled parent.

Living in the heart of the South, where had this girl formed an opinion that only a few years back would have been considered almost shocking? Perhaps not in the home at Christmas time, where Eliza and Tom and all the little pickaninnies were gathered. And yet—perhaps! The spirit of love and good-will, the spirit of the Christ-child, the spirit that can change hatred into love in a miraculously short time—such a spirit has accomplished even greater wonders.

When the Negro finally comes into his own in the South and throughout the land, he can look back and give thanks for the birthday, with all its vast significance, of the One who did not think it necessary to explain when He said, "*My* people."

The Old Shepherd's Story

By N. M. YLVISAKER

Illustrated by R. J. Norman

IT happened long, long ago. I was only a lad then. My father was a shepherd, and he would often let me accompany him as he tended his flocks on the Bethlehem hills. The sheep we watched needed special care, for they were destined for the sacrificial services in the temple in Jerusalem. At night it was the custom among the shepherds that several of them joined so that both they and their flocks might have the protection that numbers give.

I remember one such night—remember it better than any other night in my life. We had had a hard day. The sheep were unusually restless. They needed constant watching. And when the evening shadows fell and the stars of heaven appeared, it seemed there was an unearthly, supernatural, phosphorescent glow that pervaded all. We all noticed it, but so tired were we from a busy day's labors that we must have dozed as the camp fires died down.

Suddenly we were awakened by sounds all about us that none of us had ever heard before. Like ten thousand great choirs their celestial harmonies burst forth as angels of God crowded us on all sides. What gloriously enrapturing music it was. I shall never forget its glory and in my soul I hear the echoes of its heavenly chords—always.

Then, without warning, there stood an angel of light before us, whose countenance was like a burning fire. All of us fell prostrate, but he spoke kindly and reassuringly: "Fear not: . . . unto you is born this day . . . a Savior, which is Christ the Lord." And the angelic chorus sang and sang. Louder and more distinct their chorused voices echoed over the hills of Bethlehem, till at last their hymns of praise reached their final climax, and the song of it sounded like the song that is heard before the throne of God: "Glory to God in the highest, and on earth peace, good-will toward men."

Transported we listened. In awe we worshipped. Prostrate we all fell again. For here was the open gate of heaven. God was with men. And the angels sang and sang. Their glad hosannas and hallelujahs echoed and reechoed. All the bells of heaven seemed to join in the glad refrain: "Glory, glory, glory to God!"

THIRTY years had gone by. I was already a man. I had replaced my father, who had gone to the land where angels still sing. So often I had tended my flocks by night. So often I remembered. How could one ever forget?

And then—it happened again. Only quite differently after all. One day a strange man appeared in the Jordan bottoms. At Bethlehem I heard about it and hurried to see him, for never could I forget what the angel had said. Straight from the desert he came and the desert winds and the desert loneliness had made of him a man apart. But it wasn't his appearance, striking as that seemed, that made all men hesitate before him. Like the prophets of old he strode boldly through village path and city street, and everywhere he cried, like Jonah in the long ago: "Repent ye, repent ye: for the kingdom of heaven is at hand."

Not in five hundred years had Israel heard a voice like that. There was a great stir. Everywhere men and women crowded to hear. At last the press was so great that one writer in telling about it used this remarkable language: "Then went out to him Jerusalem, and all Judæa, and all the region round about Jordan" (Matt. 3:5). Never a preacher before or since like that. And never a congregation either.

But always I was listening for some word from him that might relate itself to that night of years ago. Always I was waiting. And then one day unexpectedly it came. We had been listening raptly to the remarkable preaching of John the Baptist—for it was he, of course. We knew it was true as we listened, as Jesus later said about him, "Among them that are born of women there hath not risen a greater than John the Baptist" (Matt. 11:11).

THEN from nowhere, it seemed, there came a man, passing by. No sooner did John catch sight of Him than he abruptly ceased his preaching and, stretching forth his arm in prophetic gesture, he exclaimed, as in awed silence we gave ear: "Behold the Lamb of God, which taketh away the sin of the world" (John 1:29).

Startled I listened—and then at once I knew, and understood. Here was the angel-herald's message again, the same message which had been stamped indelibly upon my memory that Christmas night of long ago: "For unto you is born a Savior." All of us know from childhood that "Lamb-of-God" and "Savior" are terms which mean the same, when God declares to our people the coming salvation.

Here was One I must follow. Together with two of John's disciples I joined the company which from this day began to follow the man from Nazareth. I saw this Man and what He did. I heard Him speak as no man had ever spoken, and with authority. The miracle happened, and all Israel followed Him. Wonders, such as had not been done since the earth was made, were accomplished before our very eyes. His words went to the soul, and sinners poured out their sins before Him—and were forgiven. God had visited His people, and His Son walked among us each day.

I COULD not help noticing that He soon selected a group of men to be with Him constantly. He evidently had a particular purpose in calling them as He did, and in teaching them carefully the things pertaining to the Kingdom. Instinctively He seemed to know what was in these men. He understood their inner being. He looked into their souls and knew how they would eventually measure up to the purposes of God—after He had changed them. So He chose.

Amazed and fascinated I watched Him as He made His selections. He spoke to two men, John and Andrew, disciples of John the Baptist. So stirred were they by the experience that one of them immediately brought to Jesus his brother, Simon Peter, who became a third disciple and apostle.

These were all unusual men. Andrew was always the active missionary. He found the boy who had the loaves

ST. JOHN

By Andrea del Sarto

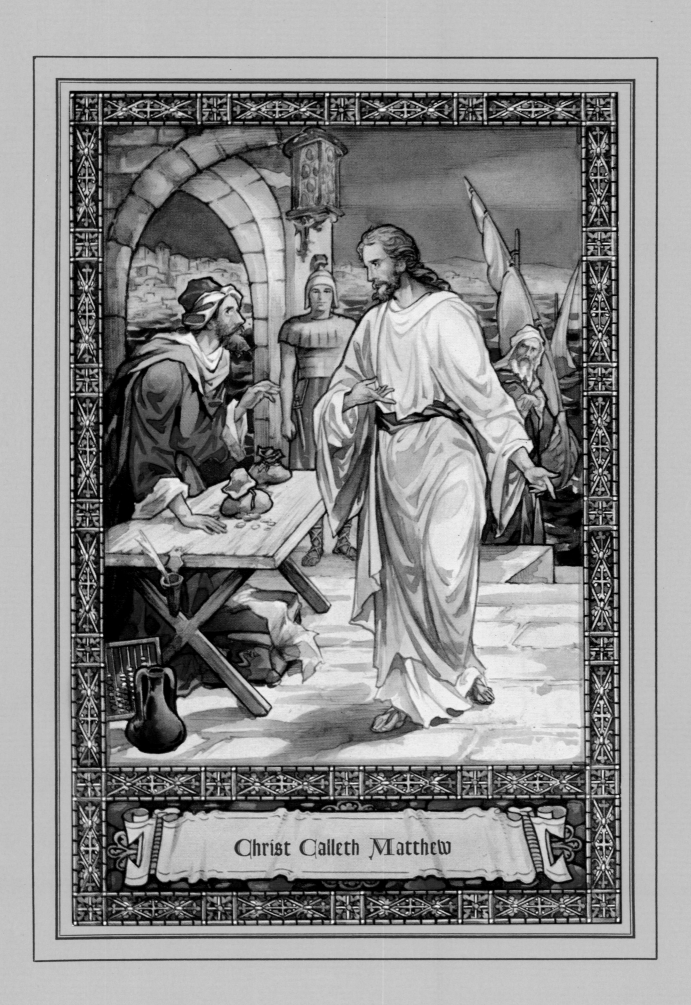

Christ Calleth Matthew

Peter   Andrew   James, Elder   Bartholomew   Philip   Thomas   James, Minor

of bread and the basket of fish, which Jesus used to feed the multitude. He brought the Greeks to Jesus, and Jesus used that experience to tell about His world embracing redemptive work.

John, the Galilean, son of Salome, brother of James the Elder, and relative of Jesus, was the fiery son of thunder. Jesus changed him and he became the great apostle of love, whom Jesus Himself loved above all the others. To him Jesus, in His last extremity on the cross, entrusted the care of His own mother.

Simon Peter, son of Jonah, the impetuous but vacillating fisherman from Bethsaida, Jesus called, and, seeing the sterling qualities that would be his when faith had made him strong, He changed his name to Cephas and made him the confessing apostle: "Thou art the Christ, the Son of God." He took him with Him into the holies of His intimate presence, and through all these experiences, including

his fall from grace, He made him a flaming witness for the truth, one of the greatest Christian messengers of all time.

And then He called Philip, the perplexed Philip, who so often questioned what he saw, but who finally became a great missionary. Philip told Nathanael, called Bartholomew, about Jesus—Nathanael in whom there was no guile, who when he understood who Jesus was could exclaim and say, as he accepted the call to apostleship: "Rabbi, thou art the Son of God; thou art the King of Israel."

ONE day I saw Jesus stop suddenly before the most unexpected place—a tax collector's booth. What did He want there? I was soon to know. He saw a young man sitting there, who held office as collector of customs and taxes, one of the most despised jobs in all the land. But Jesus saw more than the job. He saw the man. Deep down into

Matthew   Mark   Luke   John   Paul   Simon   Judas   Matthias

Matthew's soul He looked. And then He spoke. Only two words. But they went deep. "Follow me," He said—so very simply. Matthew looked up, saw Jesus, and rising up immediately, he left all and followed Him. Two words. But they changed a life. Matthew became one of the greatest apostles, and this tax collector was later entrusted with the sacred task of giving the world the written message about Jesus, the Messiah of the Jews.

Then in rapid succession Jesus joined those other men to Him: James the Elder, son of Zebedee and Salome, brother of John, the evangelist, whose selfishness at times jarred the Master. But gradually his character changed and he became one of the most trusted of all the apostles, a powerful witness for the truth, and a great preacher of the Gospel. Thomas Didymus, the man of despair, was called, and gradually skepticism was changed into confident assurance which made him exclaim, when he saw the risen Savior face to face: "My Lord and my God!"

Simon Zelotes, the Canaanite, the religious enthusiast, Jesus purged of all selfish enthusiasm and made him enthusiastic for the Kingdom of God and the true Israel that is to be. James the Less, son of Alphaeus, little known and little appreciated, a quiet, unobtrusive personality, who thought little about James but much about Christ, was made the representative of all those quiet and humble disciples, who, forgetting self, become great in the Kingdom of God. Judas Lebbeus, called Thaddaeus, the frank, open-minded follower, of whom little is known, except this question (John 14:22): "Lord, how is it that thou wilt manifest thyself unto us, and not unto the world?" received from Jesus the light which made him always want to make plain the way of the Master.

AND then there was Judas Iscariot! Why Jesus called him, I do not know. For he only hurt his Lord by his stubborn unbelief and his fearful sin at last. Perhaps we need the warning of the apostle who was called, who fell, and who was lost, lest pride of life overcome us and make us forget the glories of the message that the angels brought to earth.

All these men, but the one—and he was later replaced by Matthias—saw the Christ, heard His glorious message of salvation, learned to know Him as the Christ of God and the object of the herald-angel's evangel. They saw Him live; they saw Him die according to the Scriptures; they saw Him raised from the dead; they saw Him go back to heaven. They felt the Spirit's presence on Pentecost Day. They were filled with His power. They went out to preach His Gospel everywhere. And they changed a world.

Now I know that it was true, as the angel had said, that this Jesus should be a Savior to all people, and that the Christmas Gospel should make joyful even those who lived afar off.

NOW I am growing old, and for me the sun of life must soon set. You want to know what happened to all these faithful witnesses of the Christ of the Bethlehem manger, to what lands they brought the Christmas Gospel, and how they died.

But first we must mention the greatest apostle of them all, Paul the pharisee. Called as one out of due season, he, who had been the persecutor, became the passionate witness and missionary. He was called especially as the missionary to the Gentiles and ardently he worked and to distant lands he traveled to preach the Gospel and establish the Christian Church: through Syria, Asia Minor, Macedonia, Greece, Italy—missionary journey after missionary journey. Often he had with him the Greek physician Luke, and, strangely enough—I do not know exactly the reason why—it was left to Luke to tell to posterity our strange experiences of that first Christmas night, when the angels sang and God told us about the Savior who was born. I don't know if Luke was with Paul when he died. But Paul died in Rome, a martyr's death for his Lord.

Andrew did most of his missionary work in Jerusalem, but he died a martyr in Achaia. John labored and preached throughout Asia Minor, writing a Gospel and four other books about his Lord. While he was in exile on the isle of Patmos, he wrote that great book about coming things. He died at Ephesus in Asia Minor, the only one of the apostles, so they tell me, to die a natural death.

Simon Peter became, after his experience with Cornelius, another great traveling missionary. Through Antioch and Syria he went, perhaps even reaching Babylon. Rumor has it that he died a martyr in Rome, though that has never been verified. His disciple, Mark, curiously enough, was called by the Spirit to pen one of the four Gospels, the one in which Christ is pictured to the Romans as the strong Son of God.

Philip did missionary work in Asia Minor, where he witnessed powerfully against all idolatry and died a martyr's death. Nathanael-Bartholomew died a martyr in Armenia. James the Elder was the first martyr, being slain by Herod Agrippa because of his fearless preaching. Matthew preached in Jerusalem at first, later becoming the apostle to Africa, where he brought the message of the Savior to Ethiopia and to Egypt, and finally suffering martyrdom.

Thomas labored in Parthia, Persia, and possibly in India —at any rate we have been told that he died a martyr there. Simon Zelotes worked in Egypt and in Persia. He was sawed in two as he witnessed for his Lord. James the Less, who greatly resembled his Lord in physical appearance, met death at the hands of a revengeful mob. Judas Thaddaeus showed in all his work how necessary is the power of the Spirit.

AND now I am old, very old. I heard with my own ears the sweetest story that has ever been told. I knew John the Baptist, I saw, heard, and followed the Christ. I have told you briefly what I know of those remarkable men who were to establish and who have now built the Kingdom of God on earth.

Often as I watch the flocks I think of all the wonders I have seen and heard. But I always think I can hear the echoes of the angels' song. Always it seems the herald-angel will come again. Perhaps he will come soon. I can hardly wait. I am sure he will come. And when he comes, it will be to usher me into that upper glory, where Jesus Christ, my Savior, is. And there I *know* I shall hear again that chorused choir as with transported voices they sing again the "Glory, glory, hallelujah" I heard so long ago out on the hills of Bethlehem.

Oh, the rapture of that singing! How I long to sing the refrain with them. How I long to see my Christ and my God! Perhaps they will let me join the angel choir, and then—glory of all glories—my voice shall sing out, as did theirs that Christmas night, long, long ago: "Glory to God in the highest"—to God who was willing to save even me!

Christ Calleth Peter and Andrew

Keeping Christmas at Uncle Jothan's

By LOIS LENSKI
Illustrations by the Author

Nose, nose, jolly red nose,
And what gave me that jolly red nose?
Nutmegs and cinnamon, spices and cloves,
And they gave me this jolly red nose!

NOT nutmegs and cinnamon, nor yet spices and cloves, but a long day's ride on the stage-coach, Patience decided. She blew into her hands, trying to warm her nose with her breath, but she felt it getting colder and redder every minute. What would Uncle Jothan say? She put her hands back into her muff and patted affectionately the little paper-covered book she carried there —the book that told her about the "jolly red nose" and many other things, the well-thumbed Mother Goose which father had brought from Boston and given her for her birthday.

Would the day never end? Would the snow never stop? Would the stage never reach Winton? The long journey from New Haven, starting at daybreak, seemed endless to eight-year-old Patience. What would the farm house be like? And how would she know all the little cousins when she had never seen them? And would she be homesick, as mother had predicted, or want to remain, as father had said, and be one of Aunt Betsey's children?

The stage-coach crawled along slowly through the snow drifts and Patience wondered what "keeping Christmas" would be like. Being meeting-house people instead of church people, her parents had always kept Thanksgiving

instead. Uncle Jothan *must* be nice, since he was mother's own brother, even if he *had* married an Episcopalian. And mother always said of Aunt Betsey, "Well, if she reads her Bible, and is good to the poor and speaks no evil, why, let 'er have her Christmas; what's the harm on't? 'Taint popery, when it's Aunt Betsey."

And father said of Aunt Betsey, "She's the salt of the earth an' she likes her Christmas just the same as we like our St. Pumpkin's Day! That's what *she* calls our Thanksgiving! You just go along for it'll help your education to find out fer yourself what Christmas is like."

PATIENCE'S thoughts were interrupted by a loud blast of the horn and a noisy "Whoa!" from the red-faced stage driver. The stage stopped abruptly and in a moment the driver lifted Patience carefully out of her straw and untied her small horse-hair trunk from the "boot" at the back. The other passengers, who had become firm friends from suffering uncomplainingly all the ups and downs of the journey, grinned affectionately out of the coach door and called good-natured goodbyes. It was snowing again, softly and gently.

Patience was so stiff in her joints, so hungry, tired, and cold, she could hardly stand. She looked around in the white blur and began to pick her uncertain way to the lighted door of the inn. Just then she heard the sound of

sleigh-bells and almost at once a tall, strange man picked her up in his arms.

"I'm your Uncle Jothan!" a loud voice boomed. "And you're Patience! I'd 'a' know'd ye anywheres, day er night. Ye're the very picture o' yer mother, I kin see that!"

In another moment Patience was bundled up in buffalo robes and blankets in the sleigh, moving swiftly in the direction of the farm house down the road.

A few moments later Uncle Jothan stopped the horse in the lane by the north parlor door. It was standing open and there was Aunt Betsey with arms outstretched, and behind her a group of faces. Patience knew all the names —Kitty and Jenny and Philip and Samuel—but which was which? And Joanna, the "help," the daughter of a farmer neighbor. And Grandmother Shelton—Aunt Betsey's mother, a brand-new grandmother for Patience—where was she? Aunt Betsey gave her a big hug, which won her heart at once, and so did Joanna, before she hurried off to the kitchen, saying:

"Her nose is like an icicle, poor lambie; we'll have to get something inside o' 'er quickly."

PATIENCE thought she had never seen such a large room before; it faded off into dark corners in all directions. Candles were burning about the great center fireplace, and glowing logs sent out a welcome warmth. Several pots, from which appetizing smells arose, hung from pot hooks on a long iron crane. In a large, straight chair on the right sat a very old lady wearing a huge ruffled cap, which kept bobbing up and down over furiously clicking knitting needles.

Patience sank into a chair exhausted. The fire baked her face, but her back was still cold and her feet like chunks of ice. Afterward she had no memory of what she was given to eat at the big table with the red-checkered table cloth. But a hazy recollection of Aunt Betsey and Joanna busily ladling something out of a boiling pot, and of four pairs of eyes shyly watching her from various corners of the room, never left her.

Then, suddenly, all the others had disappeared and she was left alone with Aunt Betsey to undress by the fire. Aunt Betsey found her a woolen night-gown in her trunk and borrowed a knitted night-cap of Kitty's to keep her ears warm. Joanna wrapped a warm blanket around her and carried her upstairs to a cold, cold bedroom. Aunt Betsey walked ahead with a flickering candle and the long-handled brass warming-pan filled with hot coals from the open fire.

Patience began to shiver again, for the room seemed almost as cold as the out-of-doors. The storm, which had lulled during the sleigh-ride from the tavern, began again in great earnest. The wind rushed and howled about the house, shrieking and calling, determined to get in. A great deal of it *did* get in, through the cracks at the windows, and set the bed-curtains blowing nearby. The huge bed-stead seemed to fill the tiny room. Its posts touched the ceiling. Its length reached from wall to wall. There was only space for a tiny rug and a high-boy near the entrance door.

Aunt Betsey set the candle on the chest and proceeded to warm the bed with the warming pan. Joanna squeezed past the foot of the bed to fit in some wooden wedges to keep the windows from rattling. Then they said goodnight after cautioning their little visitor to say her prayers at once and to make haste to get into bed after blowing out the candle.

54

ONCE alone, Patience took a look about her. She had never had a room to herself before and it made her feel very grown-up and important; so, hugging her blanket tightly about her, she began to explore. Where and how to say her prayers was a problem. The bed was so high, made up with two feather beds, that a little two-step ladder was provided, which could slip underneath and out of sight in the daytime. It was almost like climbing a haystack in summer, Patience thought, as she perched on the top step and folded her hands, leaning against the soft coverings.

> Lord, if Thou lengthen out my days,
>   Then let my heart so fixed be
> That I may lengthen out Thy praise,
>   And never turn aside from Thee.
>
> And when my days on earth shall end
>   And I go hence and be no more,
> Give me eternity to spend,
>   My God to praise forevermore.
>
> Now I lay me down to take my sleep,
>   I pray the Lord my soul to keep.
> If I should die before I wake,
>   I pray the Lord my soul to take. Amen.

Pulling the blanket over her shoulders, Patience jumped up on top of the haystack and perched there. Being grown-up is doing just what you please—blowing the candle out whenever you feel like it—staying outside the covers, no matter how cold you are—listening to the whistling wind and not being afraid....

A WAVY glass over the high-boy was tipped so that she could see the upper part of her face, cut off short at the middle of her nose. Her well-known fair hair was completely covered by the borrowed night-cap's flapping ruffles—eyebrows, lashes, and ruffles seemed to float about in all directions. Patience stared in dismay at the unusual apparition. She wondered who it was. Frightened for a moment, then the humor of the situation struck her. There flashed through her mind a verse from her well-loved book:

> She began to wonder and she began to cry,
> "Lauk a mercy on me, this can't be I!
> But if it be I, as I do hope it be,
> I've a little dog at home, and he'll know me!"

Then with a laugh, and suddenly realizing that she was very cold, she tumbled under the covers and pulled them up to her neck. But the candle wasn't half burned yet, nor was Patience sleepy. She peeped out between the bed curtains, and then she saw the wall-paper.

Wide-eyed, she stared. It was like a page from a wonderful book, and all the pictures were in color. It was Noah's ark come true, straight from the Bible. There was the ark and Mr. and Mrs. Noah and the two elephants and the two bears and all the other animals; and another ark and another and another. She began to count them, and then she saw the funniest thing of all, at the crack where the wall-paper was joined—a tiger with an elephant's trunk; a bear with an ostrich's head; a lion with the long neck of a giraffe! What a wonderful room.

The candle began to flicker. She blew it out with a whiff. Wind, storm, fatigue, and all the strange newness of her surroundings forgotten, she dropped off to sleep, dreaming that she was Mrs. Noah.

55

IT seemed to Patience that she had been at Uncle Jothan's for months, when, in reality, it was less than two weeks. During this time she entered into every activity of the busy household and was accepted and truly felt herself as one of the family. Life at the farm house, with four new cousins, left her little time for homesickness, and, besides, she must find out about this mysterious event called Christmas.

One morning she was aroused from sleep and her Noah's ark dreams by disturbing sounds from below-stairs; and before she was dressed, she knew from the hustle and bustle that important events were under way. She hurried down the steep, narrow stairs, and there was grandmother sitting on the wrong side of the fireplace!

Grandmother moved! Grandmother, who belonged to the fireplace as much as the kettle or the tongs; grandmother, who could not leave her chair even when the largest logs were being carried in; grandmother who seemed to grow there, for nobody had ever seen her go to bed or get up again. Last in her place at night and first in her place in the morning, as inevitable as the big grandfather clock on the stair landing, or the steeple on the meeting house—it was unbelievable. Sitting on the left side of the fireplace instead of the right, she looked strange and different, and in her astonishment Patience nearly forgot to say good-morning. But grandmother, whose duty it was to remind children of their manners, did not let her forget for long.

Yes, grandmother noticed everything. Why, even Uncle Jothan said she had eyes in the back of her head! Especially did she notice dropped stitches and tangled threads and mumbled words in memorized texts, as well as wrong notes in the singing of hymns.

Though great events were afoot today, the lessons for Patience and Kitty, aged seven, and little four-year-old Philip, went on just the same; while Jenny and Samuel, the older children, on holiday from school, were helping busily. Two strange faces appeared in the kitchen, Joanna's sister and brother, Phoebe and Phineas.

DURING breakfast, Patience felt her face growing hotter and hotter; and the heat continued to increase until she could scarcely keep her thoughts on her food, which lay untouched on her plate. During the family prayers, Uncle Jothan took up the Bible and read the story of Nebuchadnezzar's fiery furnace, seven times heated. Right in the middle of it—she could contain herself no longer—Patience jumped off her splint-bottomed chair and shouted, "It's the oven! It's the oven!"

True enough it was, for she had been sitting right in front of it, and if she had not jumped up when she did, well might she sooner or later have been mistaken for a roasted sausage or a mince pie! But a break in family prayers was unheard-of, so Patience had to sit on a footstool at grandmother's knee and listen to a sermon on the duty of sending *all* her thoughts heavenward while praying; and then, as punishment, add an extra row of knitting to her stint for the day.

Joanna and Aunt Betsey had been up since daybreak, and, with the help of Phoebe, many preparations were under way. Jenny and Samuel had the night before brought in light-wood enough for kindling and dry hardwood for firing the big oven. Joanna had set the sponge for the bread and by breakfast time it was ready to be moulded.

No one could manage the oven like Aunt Betsey, who, long before breakfast, had filled it with wood and lighted it with a shovelful of coals from the open hearth. When the wood burned down, the hickory coals lay in a great glowing mass on the oven bottom, and Patience and Kitty and Philip had a good peep at the brilliant light cast over the vaulted brick top, as they stood up to recite the day's text in unison. Skillfully Aunt Betsey drew out the hot coals with a long-handled "peel," placing them in the compartment under the oven. Then she swept the stone floor of the oven clean with a wet corn-husk broom.

"Joanna! Joanna! Fetch the bread quickly!"

JOANNA brought the bread and Aunt Betsey placed the loaves on the stones by means of a flat wooden shovel. Phoebe followed with the pies—mince, pumpkin, and apple—which had been waiting behind the closed door of the cold buttery for this auspicious moment. Jenny and Samuel appeared as if by magic. Lessons were forgotten, and in the excitement even grandmother forgot to say, "Take heed!" All held their breath at the array of good things—which included gingerbread and seed-cakes, as well as loaves of cake with raisins.

The seed-cakes and gingerbread baked quickly and had to be taken out first, so Aunt Betsey stayed near by. What an exciting fragrance filled the room when she opened the door for inspection! The children could not help sniffing.

Patience dropped stitches all morning, and neither grandmother's advice on the subject of a little girl's usefulness, nor her verbal directions on the correct way to shape a knitted stocking were of much help. The thought of all the good things in preparation or already awaiting the great day was as disturbing as Thanksgiving at home. Only at home she was allowed to run about and watch it all without restriction. It was hard to have to sit still and think about the joys of knitting during the inactive decline of life, when one was so anxious to be active at the moment. Patience had the wicked feeling that knitting would never become for her a "never-failing amusement," as grandmother predicted, but that she was going to hate it as long as she lived, and, like those ignorant and unuseful persons grandmother so often mentioned, "go down in misery to the grave." She dropped another stitch....

CHRISTMAS Day dawned bright and clear. The snow had settled into a glistening sheet of white and was packed hard for sleighing. Two bronze-colored oxen, hitched to the big ox-sled, carried the whole family to church, the dinner being so arranged that no one would be kept from attending service. Samuel and Phineas brought out the foot-stoves, filled with hot coals, at the last moment, and tucked everyone in behind the great buffalo robes. Then with the call, "All ready!" the slowly moving beasts started their journey down hill, Uncle Jothan driving and Phineas walking at their heads.

On the whole, Patience was disappointed. There was nothing very special about this wicked Christmas, after all. Though she had never been to a Christmas service before, it did not seem different to her, even if it was " 'Piscopal." She noticed some pine branches up in front, but the reading of the prayers was much the same as at home in the meeting-house, and the sermon longer, if anything. Joanna dozed and nodded, and grandmother had to pinch her arm gently, for fear she might snore, or attract the tithing man with his feathered rod to his duties.

Little Philip, who was always hungry, had filled his pockets with raisins, gathered secretly from the kitchen. He sat on a footstool and munched them loudly. No one objected, as he could not be seen. The square, box-shaped pew with its high sides hid all the children from view—all except Jenny and Samuel, who were tall enough to see over, when the congregation stood up.

Patience was wondering what the minister looked like, having pictured him as a man with white whiskers, something like Jehovah in her Primer, or Noah on the wall-paper—when suddenly she gave a loud sneeze. Reaching for her handkerchief in her reticule, she found she had neglected to bring one, so she leaned over to ask Aunt Betsey for hers. Aunt Betsey, who was absorbed in the sermon and who disapproved of whispering in church, only shook her head and frowned.

So sneeze followed sneeze and Patience felt they were loud enough to wake the dead in the graveyard outside. Grandmother whispered, "That's enough!" and rapped her so sharply with her knuckles that it scared all future sneezes away. In the silence which ensued, Patience was surprised to hear the sermon still dragging on, as if it had no end.

But it did end at last, and so did the hymns and prayers. Whereupon little time was wasted in conversation with the other church members, as many of them, who were Aunt Betsey's "'Piscopal" relations, were expected at the farm house for dinner. During the long journey home uphill in the ox-sled, Patience and Kitty and Philip ran behind, jumping on the sled whenever they grew tired. It seemed the slowest journey in the world, because everyone wanted to hurry.

IN the early morning, Phineas and Samuel had started hickory fires in both the north and the south parlors, for the whole house was thrown open on this day, when the great feast of the year was spread. Uncles, aunts, and cousins began to arrive in large numbers, by sled, sleigh, or on horseback. Jenny and Patience met them one by one at the north parlor door, closing it promptly after each arrival, to keep the cold out, and showing the guests where to deposit their wraps.

One gay young man patted Patience on the back and said, "Is this our straight-laced Puritan from New Haven? What're ye celebratin' Christmas fer?" and laughed loudly.

The long dining table was lengthened to its uttermost. Grandmother Shelton, resplendently dressed in her new black ruffled silk taffeta, shaking her new cap-border of Dutch lace gaily, sat in her unnatural position on the wrong side of the fireplace and attained thereby an added dignity. Beyond a doubt, she held the center of the stage, and all the party, large and small, paid her homage.

"Patience, show yer Aunt Eliza where t' put her bonnet and shawl.... Ye're han'some enough, Melissa, without lookin' in the mirror an' blushin'.... Boys, put on some hickory logs in the north parlor, I feel a draft.... Now, Jerusha, it'd be better t' hear yer comments on the sermon o' the day instead o' yer new millinery outfits.... Don't forget that last dash o' seasoning the next time ye baste th' turkey, Joanna. ... Fetch the cheeses, now, from the butt'ry, Jenny, one fer each end o' the table.... There, now, Philip, you an' Kitty go help Patience with the splint-bottom'd chairs from overhead, an' mind ye don't bump into the gran'father clock...."

AT the right moment, the great oven gave up its burden of wild turkey, pork and ham and chicken pies, which had been sizzling to a turn while the household's thoughts were turned heavenward. Everything was timed to the minute and by some miracle nothing came out either burned or underdone. The pots and kettles in the fireplace, laden with an abundance of good vegetables of all sorts, called aproned aunts and cousins to their rescue with spoons and ladles. Uncle Benjamin who had been romping gaily with the girls and younger children, was called to a halt, along with his frivolous antics. Grandmother's chair was moved to the end of the table nearest the fireplace and Uncle Jothan took his place at the other end. All stood with folded hands and bowed heads while the head of the house said grace.

The table fairly groaned under its heavy load—for besides the hot meats and vegetables, there were cold tongue, sausages, ham, spare-ribs, and many other delicacies, such as cidar-apple-sauce, home-made cheeses, pickled samphire, stewed quinces, custards, apple tarts, seed-cakes, and cookies, on down to pies of various kinds and a great boiled Indian pudding. All the food was put on the big table at once and everybody ate until he reluctantly made up his mind to stop. No child properly trained might leave a portion uneaten, and, though Patience tried her best, she was not the only one who wondered what had become of her appetite and why it was she could eat no more.

IN the middle of the feast Uncle Jothan arose and said, "Now we will have intermission and exchange places."

Outside the weather had grown colder and inside the fire had grown hotter, so those who were sitting on the fire side of the table were invited to get up and carry their plates with them around to the cold side of the table; while those who had sat there were as glad to bring their plates around to the fire side to get warm.

"Here we go 'round the mulberry bush," chanted Uncle Benjamin.

"Now ye're all topsy-turvy, and I can't tell one from t'other!" cried grandmother. For she alone stayed where she was, ever the immovable, the unchangeable. A fire screen was brought and placed between the fire and her seat, to ward off the heat.

As the food disappeared, the jollity and laughter increased. Before tackling the pudding and pies, the three uncles, Jothan, Benjamin and Ebenezer, stood by the fireside and sang ballads. It was Aunt Jerusha who smelled their burning coat-tails and advised them it was time to stop. Whereupon grandmother surprised everyone by announcing suddenly, "Now it's my turn! I will sing 'The Miser'!"

> A rich old miser courted me,
> His age was three score years and three,
> And I a girl of seventeen,
> I wish his face I'd never seen!

The quavering old voice sang with great gusto and dramatic flourish, and brought forth a round of appreciative clapping.

Food forgotten at last, a hymn was sung, and afterward Uncle Jothan rose at the head of the table and spoke a friendly prayer, thanking the Father for His many gifts and for His special gift on this day, the Babe in the manger, and asking a remembrance for all Absent Friends before the Throne of Grace.

SUDDENLY, then, the great feast was over. Chairs were pushed back and the table cleared with speed by many helping hands. Uncle Benjamin started a game of "blindman's-bluff" in the south parlor to take the children out from under foot.

By the time the women had washed the dishes and put the house in order, dusk began to fall. Aunt Betsey brought out the best tallow candles, which she had made especially for the purpose, and young and old crowded as close as they could around the fire. A feeling of expectancy filled the air.

Gifts for the children appeared as if by magic. A pincushion with her name on it, all spelled out in pins, surrounded by a prickly border of flowers designed in the same style, for Kitty; a hand-whittled doll, dressed up in sprigged calico, for Patience; russet for a new petticoat for Aunt Betsey; a brightly-painted tin horse for little Philip; *The Looking-Glass, Short Stories with a Moral,* for Jenny; a Latin grammar for Samuel; linen cambric for ruffles and lawn for kerchiefs, bright buttons for small boys' jackets, small packages of much prized tea and other spices for various adults; an austere-looking volume, *The Whole Duty of Man,* for Uncle Jothan, and many other treasures; ending with nuts, raisins and precious oranges for all.

BEFORE the party broke up, one last ceremonial game was played. All the doors of the connecting rooms being set open, children and grown-ups joined hands and merrily encircled the great chimney—that warm hearth and firm buttress of the home—and grandmother, too, and danced merrily about and in and out, singing, "Oats, Peas, Beans and Barley Grows." Then, finally, coming to a standstill, young and old crowded around grandmother on all sides to sing the final verse, "Now you are married, you must obey!"

Grandmother blushed and shook her border-cap in faint embarrassment under the pointed fingers of her loved ones. A final game of tag provided a general hullaballoo till all were out of breath and greatly flustered, a last frolic to precede the putting on of bonnets and shawls and a general departure.

And then, suddenly, the house was quiet again and strangely empty, and the size of the family had dwindled to nothing at all. Patience sat down on a footstool at grandmother's knee and asked softly:

"Grandmother, is it goin' to church instead o' meetin', or helpin' with the dinner, or th' Babe in the manger, or havin' gifts fer everybody, or, what is it, 'keepin' Christmas'?"

"Why, it's all o' 'em put together, lambie," said grandmother, "so now ye know what Christmas is!"

THE STAR OVER BYZANTIUM
(Continued from page 40)

"It is about the Greek," said the spokesman. "Our Lord is not pleased. Never has it stormed like this on Christmas Eve. We insist that you send him out."

"Your Lord and my Lord, Jesus, was never angry when one fed a friend or an enemy," replied Philip. "Did ye never read His words, 'For I was hungry and ye gave me meat; I was thirsty and ye gave me drink; I was hungry and ye took me in'? Surely our Lord would not be angry because of Theodore."

"Then why the storm?" growled the man.

"Yes, why the storm?" others echoed.

Then they stopped. The sky was clearing. Already one bright star could be seen in the heavens. Like a beacon it threw its ray on the partition in the tent. The squire drew the curtains apart. The light of the star rested upon the sleeping boy.

MOTIONED by Philip, the soldiers drew near and watched the youth. His breath was even and deep. His face showed no signs of hate or fear.

"God has spoken indeed, Philip. We yield to Him. It is His star."

They kneeled in prayer and then silently left the tent.

Philip awakened the Greek lad.

"The hour has come," he said. "The sky is clear. Now go to your home, carrying the love of the Lord of both Latin and Greek. Visit the little manger in the church tomorrow and pray for me. Think of us when you hear the choirs sing, 'Peace on earth, good-will toward men.'"

> The Holy Supper is kept, indeed,
> In whatso we share with another's need;
> Not what we give but what we share,
> For the gift without the giver is bare;
> Who gives himself with his alms feeds three,
> Himself, his hungering neighbor, and me.
>
> —JAMES RUSSELL LOWELL

Messenger of Mercy on Lonely Labrador

By ARCHER WALLACE

ON Easter Sunday in 1908, which fell on April 21st, it was still severe winter weather at Saint Anthony's in northern Newfoundland. Everywhere there was snow and ice. Out in the ocean the sea was frozen for miles, although the break-up was daily expected.

After the morning service at a little church, a boy came running to Dr. Grenfell with the news that some men and a large team of dogs had arrived from a settlement sixty miles to the south with the hope that the doctor would go back with them to visit a young man who was suffering from bone disease of the thigh and was sorely in need of the doctor's help. Dr. Grenfell agreed to go at once. He made ready the dogs that had pulled him across hundreds of miles of snow and ice: Moody, Watch, Spy, Brin, Jerry, Sue and Jack—all magnificent beasts and never happier than when hauling a komatik over the frozen wastes.

The men who had come for Dr. Grenfell were anxious to travel back with him but in the first twenty miles the doctor's dogs traveled so fast that on two or three occasions he had to wait until the others caught up. On the morning of the second day the doctor sent the others ahead with their dogs two hours before he left, feeling sure that he would soon catch up.

A deep bay had to be crossed; to go around by the shore would mean a tiresome and dangerous journey over huge boulders that lay on the land-wash. While the bay was still frozen, clear water could be seen a mile away. This was a sure sign that the spring break-up had come at last, and Dr. Grenfell knew that if he did succeed in crossing the bay it would be the last time for that season.

HE set off with his dogs at a fast pace. The ice was rough but appeared strong, although to the east could be heard terrific noises as immense blocks of ice were being smashed by the incoming Atlantic waves.

For nearly four miles all went well and there was less than half a mile to go when Dr. Grenfell perceived that he was traveling over soft "sish" ice. Terrific explosions could be heard all around and soon no pan of ice larger than ten feet square could be seen. The whole field of ice loosened so rapidly that retreat was impossible.

There was not a moment to lose. Dr. Grenfell dragged off his oilskins and threw himself on his hands and knees beside the komatik, at the same time urging the dog-team to make a dash for the shore, which was nearly a quarter of a mile away. The dogs scented danger and hesitated and the komatik sank into the soft slob ice, which made it almost impossible for them to pull and soon they sank into the water.

The doctor had securely wound the leader's trace around his wrists. About twenty-five yards away was a large cake of ice, like a huge snowball, and upon this the leading dog managed to scramble. The doctor made futile efforts to get onto this pan. Numbed and frozen with the ice water, he was beginning to feel drowsy when he noticed the trace of another dog nearby. Grasping this he was able to drag himself onto the little island of slob ice.

HE saw, however, that this piece of frozen snow was much too small for himself and the dogs and that before very long they would all be drowned. Twenty yards away was a much larger and firmer pan and he realized that if that one could be reached, it would at least postpone death for a while and give any rescuers a chance to reach him. He cut the sealskin traces from the dogs' harnesses and spliced them together to make one long line, then he removed his sealskin boots, which were full of ice and water, and tied them separately to the back of one of the dogs. He had already lost his coat, cap, gloves, and overalls.

None of the dogs seemed willing, however, to leave the small pan of ice and plunge into the water in an effort to reach the larger one. If he did push them into the water, they struggled back again.

Then he took the small, black spaniel dog which was as light as a feather and could get across without much difficulty. He showed him the direction in which to go and flung a piece of ice toward the big pan. Without a second's hesitation the spaniel dashed into the water and reached the pan safely, with one end of the line in his mouth.

The other dogs now understood what the doctor wanted and fought their way bravely through the frozen sea to the little spaniel. All but one succeeded in getting onto the new haven of refuge.

Grenfell then took a run, such as the little pan of ice would afford, and made a dive into the sea. He had taken the precaution to tie some of the harness around the dogs' bellies and after a long fight he was able to drag himself onto the new pan. He cut down his long boots as far as the foot and made a kind of jacket which shielded him from the rising wind.

THERE is probably no greater dog lover in all the world than Dr. Grenfell, but at last the situation became so desperate that he was forced to kill three of the dogs in order to have their skins for protection. He says he envied the dead beasts as they lay on the ice because their sufferings were over, while ahead of him there seemed a lingering death from starvation and exposure.

And so alone, except for the company of three dogs, the brave doctor found himself drifting steadily out to sea. It is interesting to read, in his own words, his account of that bitter moment:

"The necessity for work saved me from undue philosophizing; and night found me ten miles on my seaward voyage, with the three dogs skinned and their fur wrapped around me as a coat. I also frayed a small piece of rope into oakum and mixed it with the fat from the intestines of my dogs.

"But, alas, I found that the matches in my box, which was always chained to me, were soaked to a pulp and quite useless. Had I been able to make a fire out there at sea, it would have looked so uncanny that I felt sure that the fishermen friends, whose tiny light I could just discern twinkling away in the bay, would see it.

"The carcasses of my dogs I piled up to make a windbreak, and at intervals I took off my clothes, wrung them out, swung them in the wind, and put on first one and then the other inside, hoping that the heat of my body would thus dry them.

"My feet gave me the most trouble, as the moccasins were so easily soaked through in the snow. But I remembered the way in which the Lapps who tended our reindeer carried grass with them, to use in their boots in place of dry socks. As soon as I could sit down I began to unravel the ropes from the dogs' harnesses, and although by this time my fingers were more or less frozen, I managed to stuff the oakum into my shoes."

Among the few things he had been able to drag onto the ice-pan was a large box containing some old football clothes which he had worn at college more than twenty years earlier. Shortly he stood on the ice-pan wearing red, yellow, and black stockings of football days, and a striped flannel shirt. Half-frozen as he was, he could not help seeing the funny side of the situation.

IT was a moonlight night and he lay down beside the dogs and slept, waking every few minutes as it seemed likely his little island of ice was going to be smashed to atoms.

Then something unexpected happened. The wind seemed to die down completely and the thought came to Dr. Grenfell that he was still within sight of cottages on the mainland. As soon as daylight came he took off his flannel shirt and waved it as a flag of distress.

More than once he thought of giving up. It all seemed so ridiculous. The cliffs with the tiny cottages were miles away

and the chance of anyone's seeing him was small. He thought he saw men in the distance against the cliffs, but the objects turned out to be trees. Several times he was certain he saw a boat appearing and disappearing on the surface of the water and he kept on waving frantically in the hope of attracting attention, till it proved to be a piece of ice bobbing up and down. He had slept, however, and he felt that he could last for a good many hours yet if only the ice-pan did not melt in the sunshine.

He laid his wood and matches out in the sun to dry and was searching on the ice-pan for a piece of transparent ice which he could use as a burning glass. If he could make a fire that would last even for half an hour, the strange sight would surely attract some of the settlers on that lonely coast.

Then he saw in the distance what looked like the glitter of an oar, but he had been disappointed so often that he refused to entertain the idea that it was really a boat. A minute or two later, however, he saw it again and this time the glitter was very distinct, but as his sun glasses had been lost and he was now partially sun-blind he would not trust his vision. But the third time he saw the glint of an oar, the black of a boat's hull was visible against the ice and he knew that rescuers were near.

THE boat drew nearer and nearer until he could make out the faces of the men. They shouted to him, "Don't get excited. Keep on the ice-pan where you are." As a matter of fact, they were more excited than he. The boat drew nearer and one man leaped onto the ice-pan and grasped the doctor's hand. Not a word was spoken. The emotion of both men was too great for speech. The rescuers had thoughtfully brought with them a thermosbottle of hot tea, and soon the doctor and the dogs were hoisted on board and they started for home.

What had happened is this: The night before four men had been out on the cliffs cutting up seals which they had killed the previous fall. As they were leaving for their homes, the keen eyes of one of the fishermen detected something unusual on the ice. None of them could make out what it was, but as soon as they returned to the settlement they procured the one good spyglass on that section of the coast and hurried out to the cliffs again.

By this time it was almost dark but with the aid of the glass, they could see that there was a man on the ice and that he was frantically waving a distress signal. They guessed at once who he was and, though it was utterly impossible to rescue him in the middle of the night, as soon as dawn came a volunteer crew was organized and the boat set out, facing the heavy breakers through the ice to rescue the doctor.

WHEN Dr. Grenfell and his three dogs were safely landed at the village, every person there gave them a welcome. Writing his account of the adventure, the doctor said: "I must have looked a weird object as I stepped ashore, tied up in rags, stuffed out with oakum, and wrapped in dogskins. The news had reached the hospital that I was lost, so I at once started north for Saint Anthony, though I must confess that I did not greatly enjoy the trip, as I had to be hauled like a log, my feet being so frozen that I could not walk. For a few days subsequently I had painful reminders of the adventure, in my frozen hands and feet, which forced me to keep to my bed—an unwelcome and unusual interlude in my way of life."

"In our hallway stands a bronze tablet:

" 'To the Memory of
Three Noble Dogs
Moody
Watch
Spy
Whose lives were given
For mine on the ice
April 21st, 1908.'

"The boy whose life I was intent on saving was brought to the hospital a day or so later in a boat, the ice having cleared off the coast temporarily; and he was soon on the road to recovery."

DR. WILFRED GRENFELL made his first trip to Labrador in 1892 and so for forty-three years this doctor has been a messenger of mercy to thousands of fishermen who go annually to Newfoundland and other parts of the Atlantic coast to bleak Labrador. When he arrived there, he found more than twenty-five thousand fishermen without medical assistance of any kind. For generations there had been fishermen on the seven-hundred-mile stretch of that land—perhaps the finest cod-fishing ground in all the world—but hundreds of fishermen had died for lack of medical or surgical aid.

In addition to these Newfoundland fishermen, who visited the coast for about three months each summer, there were the people who lived on the Labrador coast the entire year. These people are called "liveyeres," meaning people who "live here." These people, who are either whites or half-breeds, have their homes at the heads of bays in winter, where they do much trapping. In the summer they visit the coast and fish. Strictly speaking, none of these people live inland. The interior is a vast and almost unexplored and uninhabited wilderness, bleak, barren, and inhospitable. In addition to the "liveyeres," there are wandering Indians known as Montagnais, and to the far north are Eskimos.

THE arrival of the *Albert* among the vessels of the fishing fleet aroused much curiosity. Vessels of traders were often seen, for these men competed with one another for the fishermen's catch. But this little vessel with the blue flag was quite different and her anchor chains had scarcely dropped before little boats were pulling toward her from a score of vessels.

The news spread like wildfire that this was a hospital ship with an English doctor on board who was willing, in fact anxious, to help everyone he could, and that he would not take any money for his services or for his medicine. He had been sent to them by the Deep Sea Mission. The news seemed almost too good to be true.

Previous to this there had been a mailboat which made a few trips during the summertime with a doctor aboard, but about all the doctor could do was to make a very hurried visit and leave a bottle of medicine. Dr. Grenfell meant to do something very different. He would live among the people, going from harbor to harbor and from home to home. He was sorely needed, and the king himself could not have been more welcome.

That first day in 1892 was a busy time for the doctor. All day long people came to see him. It seemed to him that there must be sick people on board every schooner in the harbor. The next day was much the same, only by this time

the "liveyeres" on shore had heard about this good Messenger and some brought their sick to the *Albert,* while others pleaded with him to visit those at home who could not be moved. Some of these people were seriously ill with dangerous and painful diseases. The ailments of others were trivial. Sometimes a tooth had to be extracted or perhaps a limb had to be amputated. In every case the doctor did all that lay in his power, and did it without price, which to these poor people was a great boon.

It would be impossible in this sketch to tell of all that Dr. Grenfell has done for the people of Labrador and the fishermen that go there each year, but the following incident is typical of scores which have taken place.

ONE day Dr. Grenfell was told of a family living on a lonely spot on the Labrador coast that was in great distress and needed the attention of a doctor. He went at once to the cove where stood the little building that served as a home. Surprised that no one came to offer welcome as the boat approached, he and a shipmate went ashore. Still no one appeared, nor was any smoke issuing out of the chimney. Thinking there could be no one at home, he lifted the latch and entered. A sight met his eyes which moved his heart.

Upon a bed lay the mother—dead. The father, who was a trapper, lay upon the floor, so ill that he could not move; in fact, he died that night. In the corner were five frightened little children, huddled together.

Dr. Grenfell and his crew buried the man and the woman and then took the five little children on board the ship. An uncle, living on the coast, took one child, two others were sent to a farm in New England, the other two Dr. Grenfell took to one of his hospitals.

It was this sad incident, and a number of others of a similar nature, that led Dr. Grenfell to try to raise money for an orphanage at St. Anthony, where these helpless little folks could be taken care of. The doctor just had to do something, for he was constantly obliged to take into his hospitals children who had been left without anyone to provide for them. As Dillon Wallace says, the doctor was getting to be like the old lady who lived in a shoe and had so many children she didn't know what to do.

DR. GRENFELL'S desire for a Children's Home was realized through the generosity of friends who saw the great need and came to his assistance. He conceived the brilliant idea that children of the United States, Canada, and Great Britain would be glad to assist in the erection and maintenance of the building, and he has not been disappointed. Now, in addition to the fine hospitals, there is a splendidly equipped orphanage, where during the past few years loving care has been given to hundreds of little folks who might have had to suffer untold misery had there been no such refuge for them.

Labrador remains a bleak and lonely coast. It is still lashed by the fury of Atlantic gales. But life for hundreds of folks in that land has been made brighter than it was years ago. Sick folks do not have to languish in hopeless misery as they did, nor do helpless little children there suffer untold misery as was once the case. Tremendous changes for the better have taken place, and if there is one man to whom, more than to any other, credit for all this improvement should be given, that man is Dr. Wilfred T. Grenfell.

On Christmas Day

By MARGARET W. EGGLESTON

"DING, Dong! Ding, Dong!" pealed the bell in the steeple of the village church on a Christmas Day ten years ago, and the villagers—some in sleighs, some in old-fashioned automobiles, some on foot—hurried along the country road, fearing to be late, lest they miss seeing the junior choir march in, wearing, for the first time, the vestments sent them by a city church. No loyal parishioner wanted to miss that processional.

Enoch Dane and his wife, Sarah, were among the last to arrive. The Danes were usually late. Their hillside farm was more than five miles from the church, and they had no hired help to assist them with the many things that had to be done before they could leave home. Sometimes they were late because Martha, their adopted daughter of eighteen, could not fix her curls or her hat to suit her fancy. On this Sunday, however, Martha was already at church, for she was the soloist of the junior choir. For weeks she had looked forward to the thrill of leading the procession on Christmas Day. She had pressed her vestment carefully and knew already how "sweet and pretty" she looked in it.

Enoch was well known all over that part of the state of Maine. His face, though often unshaved, was always radiant with sunshine. His ready wit and incessant stream of stories made him good company. His generosity had kept the family poor in cash but rich in friends. He was a pillar in the church. He sang in the choir, took the offering, and at times even read the service for the burial of the dead. Enoch was trying to be an earnest, sincere Christian, yet he was a constant trial to Sarah, his wife, for he was easy-going, even shiftless, in his work about the farm. The barn door had hung by one hinge for three years. The veranda, added to the house ten years ago, was still unfinished. Trees lay where they had fallen, and grass often spoiled while waiting to be cut. "Haste makes waste" was Enoch's favorite saying, and his house and farm attested it.

Enoch had inherited the farm from his ancestors. It stood on a high plateau, surrounded by hills. There was a lake within walking distance, but Enoch was the only frequent visitor there. Martha was not allowed to row or to swim, lest she be drowned. Sarah had been lame from birth and could not walk so far. The farm was a place of beauty and peace, but it was also a place of great loneliness and deprivation for Sarah and Martha. There were no labor-saving devices in house or field, though the acres of standing pine could easily have procured them. Water was drawn from the well and carried many rods to the house, though a spring on the hillside could have furnished plenty for kitchen and bath. Enoch just didn't "get at it."

SARAH DANE had not had a becoming hat or dress in the memory of any neighbor. She wore what friends or visitors gave her, regardless of style or color, and she never seemed to realize that she looked queer. Her hair was fine and curly, but she wore it drawn back tightly from her face. Sarah wasn't well and the work on the farm was hard, so she usually looked as though she would like to "set and set," as Enoch often said and did; yet she was always busy.

Sarah was surely very plain, but her real beauty could not be hidden by homely hats or unbecoming dresses; sometimes they enhanced it. Sincerity, nobility of character, and love for each and all were written in every line of her face. Sarah was the saint of the village, if there were one.

Once an artist, who came to spend the summer in the village, chanced to sit behind Sarah in church. "My!" he said to his friend, as soon as they were back in their car again, "I should like to paint the motherly face of the woman who sat in front of us. Who is she? Hers is a face one seldom sees and never forgets. There is great beauty of soul." But Sarah had neither time nor desire to have her picture painted, so she refused his request.

As she hurried into church that Christmas morning, Sarah carried a bunch of red velvet poinsettias, that she might have a part in decorating the church for the day. From early spring to late fall flowers from Sarah's garden regularly graced the pulpit and platform, though the task of picking them was always painful to her. This morning, as usual, she went directly to the altar rail, arranged the poinsettias, and reverently bowed her head in prayer.

"God," she whispered, "make me thankful for my good home and for my church. Help me to spend this day in such a manner that I may honor the birthday of Jesus, my Savior. Amen." Sarah read through the hymn as she waited for the service to begin, for she liked to sing intelligently.

SOON Enoch took his place in the choir, his genial face appearing above the singers in the front row. He didn't pray; he didn't read the hymn; he just watched the door leading into the church, lest he should miss the first glimpse of his Martha in the new vestment. When she came—her face red from the wind, and her curls awry—Enoch's face was a study in supreme satisfaction. Martha could sing well—but she knew it—and her voice soon rang out above the rest as they marched down the aisle. Martha could do well whatever she made up her mind to do, and she had chosen to be a leader in church and community. Enoch was proud of her; Sarah was not at all certain that it was good for Martha to be conscious of her ability.

Martha was the child of Sarah's sister, who had died soon after the baby was born. When the little one was found to have infantile paralysis, its shiftless father just disappeared, leaving the child to be cared for by neighbors. Because there was no one else willing to assume the responsibility, Enoch and Sarah took charge of Martha when she was not yet two years old. Years before, the Danes had buried their only little son, Benjamin, and Enoch's fatherly heart had yearned for another child to love and cherish. So, when Martha came—puny and helpless, but bright and beautiful—he opened his heart and his home with a welcome that was deep and lasting. He shared with Sarah the long, weary hours that had to be spent rubbing the withered leg. He carried her about on his shoulders until she was able to walk; and when she was old enough to go to school, he didn't complain about the four-mile ride in the old Ford each day.

Enoch adored—and spoiled—Martha. She had recovered

First Snow
a reproduction of
an original wood cut
by Herschel C. Logan

Barn in Winter
a reproduction of
an original wood cut
by Herschel C. Logan

from her illness in a remarkable way, yet, to him, she was always something to be spared, to be humored, and to be admired. So Martha, brilliant in school and active in the community, was lazy, selfish, and discontented in the home on the hillside. She wanted to go away to school, but Enoch had said he could not get the money to make it possible for her to go. Her determination to be free to do what she chose made her a serious problem to patient, gentle, faithful Sarah.

THAT beautiful Christmas morning, Sarah sincerely worshipped during the hour that she spent in the village church. Enoch's thoughts revolving about Martha, and, perhaps, also Sarah. Martha's mind was intent on a new and wonderful plan for the years ahead, though apparently she had been giving heart and soul to the singing of the old Christmas carols. She said little as they rode home through the great pine forest that lined the hill road, but when they passed a small house near the top of the hill, she furtively raised her hand to her head, lifting two fingers as a sign to a boy called Job, who was sitting in the doorway of the barn.

Some of Martha's Christmas gifts had been in her stocking that morning, but most of them were waiting for her near the Christmas tree when they reached home. There was the bright red coat and hat for which she had longed, and Enoch felt repaid for the loss of the new overcoat, which he sorely needed, when he saw her radiant face. Under the tree were several books that Sarah hoped Martha might learn to enjoy. Martha thanked with a sigh as she read the titles. Not a mystery story or a love story among them!

IT was two o'clock before they had eaten their dinner, and had enjoyed the fun of opening their Christmas gifts. When Job, the half-witted son of a neighbor, came strolling into the kitchen, Martha insisted that Sarah should join Enoch in an hour of rest while she and Job washed the dishes. Job was going to visit his sister in Texas the next day and said he had come to say goodbye. Sarah rebelled at going before the work was done, but Martha stood firm. She couldn't give them gifts, she said, but she wanted to help them and in this way express appreciation for her wonderful Christmas. So Sarah and Enoch left the young people alone.

A half hour went by. Martha peeked into the living-room every few minutes. The first time she shook her head to Job; the next time she smiled; the last time she stole quietly to her bedroom and came back with two suitcases, which she handed to Job, saying,

"Go quickly—by the lower side of the house where no one can see you. Don't come back again. Remember! Hurry!"

When Enoch and Sarah again joined her, Martha played the reed-organ for them, sang carols with Enoch, and cooked maple candy to give to Job to eat on his journey. When bedtime came, Sarah's heart was full of gratitude. Martha had been happy and contented all day.

"Dear God," said Enoch, as the two knelt in prayer, "we thank Thee for this day. We thank Thee for our home—and for Martha, who makes it so happy for us both. Help us to be faithful to each other, and to Thee. Amen."

THE next morning Martha was gone. Her old clothes lay neatly folded in the drawer. The pretty red coat and hat were missing. Her violin had been taken from its place in the hall. Boxes of powder had been dropped in her haste to get away. When he went to her room to see why she did not come downstairs to help Sarah with the breakfast, Enoch found a note on the dresser. He handed it, speechless with grief and fear, to Sarah when he came back into the kitchen.

"Dear Mother and Daddy," Sarah read aloud, "I want to learn to be a great singer. I hate the farm and I can't stay another day, especially since I have a grand chance to go now. I wanted to say goodbye to you when I went to bed, but I knew you wouldn't let me go if I told you my plans. I'm sorry to hurt you, but I have to go. Thanks for being good to me so many years. I can take care of myself now. I have taken all the money that mother left me, so I have enough until I get some work. When I know where I am to live, I'll write you, of course. I am going with Job, so don't worry. I shall get there all right. I love you both.

"Lots of kisses from Martha."

When Sarah had read the letter a second time, she put it slowly down on the table and sat down. She felt very tired. Enoch read it again to himself, walked to the stove, tore the letter into bits, and dropped them, one by one, on the glowing coals. As the last bit of paper turned to ashes, Sarah put her hand lovingly on his shoulder. She did not speak, as he walked, like one in a daze, to his bedroom door. When he came out of his room, ten hours later, Enoch looked years older. His face, always so happy and full of cheery smiles, was bitter; it was set in ugly lines.

"Sarah," he said, decisively, "Christmas, and Martha, and God have all gone out of my life together. Never mention any of them to me again. I have learned that none of them is worth what it costs."

Sarah nodded silently. She knew from experience that when Enoch had made his decision he would abide by it. But though he could keep her from talking, he could not keep her from loving and forgiving. Sarah knew well, at that moment, that she would need God in her life more than ever in the days and months ahead.

FIVE years went by—dreadful years for Enoch and Sarah. His shoulders sagged; his hair turned grey. His words were few, and usually bitter. His cruelty seared Sarah's very soul, and she worked harder, that she might think less. She felt tired and worn all the time, and sometimes she longed to be like Martha and run away from the farm. One letter had come from Martha, a few months after she had gone, but Enoch had returned it unopened, not even letting Sarah know its postmark. Occasionally their neighbor told them of Job, but Martha's name was never linked with his, and no one in the village seemed to realize that she had left with the boy. Knowing the heredity of Job's family, Sarah's heart was sick when she thought of the fate that might await Martha's children.

At first Sarah had hidden all of Martha's things, but later she had given them away, one by one, lest Enoch should chance to find them. Each Christmas she had bought a few gifts, and made the seed cakes and pumpkin pie which Martha had always wanted for Christmas, but the farm animals only had enjoyed the feast. Christmas each year was like every other day—lonely and full of regrets. Sarah would sometimes steal into the parlor and have a good cry as she looked at Martha's favorite picture, "The First Robin of

Spring." Each spring she dreaded the appearance of the first robin. "Martha! Martha!" it seemed to call, and Sarah longed intensely to hear from the girl she had cared for with such sacrifice and effort.

The old car had fallen apart, and so, each Sunday, Sarah rode alone to church in a wagon that had once been used by Enoch's ancestors, and behind an old farm horse that seemed about ready to follow the fate of the car. Church was more lonely than home, yet she went. She prayed for Enoch, and for Martha. Sometimes she wondered which of the two needed God more. Sarah's religion was her comfort and challenge; Enoch's was his goad and his torment.

IT was the sixth year after Martha's disappearance and Christmas again fell on Sunday. The snow was deep, and Sarah found it difficult to get to church. While she was away, Enoch swept the barn, moved some hay in the loft, oiled the harness, and did numerous other things that could easily have been done on Monday. Then he walked wearily to the top of the hill to meet Sarah, fearing the old horse might slip on the ice in the road and tip Sarah into the ditch.

They had eaten their dinner in silence, but as they rose, Enoch bent and kissed her, and Sarah was glad. There was still some love in his heart, and he remembered the day, she thought. A kiss had been a rare thing since Martha went.

After dinner a great snowstorm came up the valley, and the wind sent the snow in huge drifts about the farmhouse. Enoch went to the window many times and looked up the road; Sarah knew that he was restless and unhappy. At last, toward evening, he put on his sheepskin coat and fur cap. He took his snowshoes from the peg and made ready to go out.

"Don't wait up for me, Mother," he said. "I'm going to walk miles, maybe—maybe only rods. You're a good wife, Sarah—better than I deserve, I wish I could stay here with you tonight—but I can't. God must love you—even if He hates me—and Martha."

Sarah started. It was the first time she had heard him speak Martha's name. She rose, kissing him gently on the forehead, as she said,

"Enoch, God loves you—and Martha, too. I love you both, and I can forgive you both. God also forgives—and loves you, Enoch."

It seemed as though he wanted to say something. He opened the door, and shut it again. He buttoned his heavy coat nervously. He looked at her sadly, wistfully, and went out into the storm.

Sarah feared for his life as she looked across the field. She lighted a lamp and placed it in the east window; later she lighted another and put it in the west window, for she did not know the direction he had taken. She made a blazing fire in the fireplace, that it might be cozy when he returned. After two hours, she prepared a pot of coffee and a plate of cinnamon toast—a strange Christmas supper, but it was one that Enoch would surely like. Twice she tried to play some carols on the reed-organ, but tears blurred the page so that she could not read the notes. Suppose she should lose Enoch on this Christmas night, as she had lost Martha six years before! Finally she sat down by the fire that blazed brightly in the great fireplace—waiting, thinking, praying.

67

ENOCH went slowly up the hill-road until he came to an old house where his grandfather had lived when Enoch was a little boy. In the lee of the building, he was sheltered from the storm, and he was already feeling tired. Looking back at his own house, he saw the light in the eastern window.

" 'Tisn't any wonder Martha couldn't stay there when she was eighteen," he mused. "I should have seen it. That place is too lonesome for a girl. Maybe it is too lonesome for Sarah, too." He pushed his way along the drifted road till he could see the village in the other valley.

"I should have cut some pine, so that I could have sent her away to school," he said. "I was selfish. I wanted her all to myself. I should have let her bring the boys along home; but I was afraid she would leave me lonely again—as Benjamin left me lonely." He struggled on, passing the house where Job had lived. He clenched his hands, muttering:

"A half-witted man for a husband when I wanted her to have the best in the land."

In the distance he could see the spire of the church, and he was impelled to go in that direction.

"The church is never locked," he thought. "I should have gone with Sarah this morning, but I couldn't make myself say so. I'll drop in there now. Maybe Sarah is right. Maybe God forgives me—and Martha, too. Maybe I ought to have forgiven Martha long ago. Sarah looked old and tired today. I'm sorry I haven't been kind to her. Sarah is a good woman."

ENOCH turned the curve in the road. It was down hill all the way to the church from that point, so he hurried along. Suddenly he almost ran into a woman who was struggling up the hill. She was carrying a heavy bundle, and seemed almost exhausted.

"If that was any woman but Mrs. Mallet," he thought, "I would stop and help her, but she is always doing some silly thing like this. She ought to know better than to go out in such a storm." And he pushed aside trying to pass her unnoticed, as she bent her head against the wind.

There was a cry, as of great pain, and the woman fell, headlong, into the snow, her bundle rolling to one side of the road. Thinking she must be seriously hurt, Enoch ran to help her. He put his strong arm under hers, saying, as he knelt beside her:

"I'll help you, Mrs. Mallet. No woman should try to battle a storm like this."

"Daddy!" she cried. "Don't you love me any more, Daddy? Forgive me for coming home, but I couldn't stay away another Christmas Day. Please forgive me."

Enoch trembled. He felt as though he, too, were going to fall. He released his grip on her arm and rose to his feet, unsteadily. Martha had come home! What should he do?

"Look, Daddy," she said, feebly trying to crawl across the snow to her bundle, "I have brought little Enoch to you. He needs a father. His father is . . ." but she could not say the awful word. She put her head down on the snow and sobbed as though her heart would break. She was not wanted; she was not loved.

ENOCH stood as one transfixed. Martha had come. This was Martha's baby! Job's baby! But where was Job? Had he sent Martha back to the farm? He awkwardly pushed aside the blanket that covered the face of the child. It reminded him of Martha when she came to him—motherless, fatherless, in need of love. The child smiled at him, but Enoch drew away. Martha saw—and feared to hear him speak.

"Daddy!" she cried, trying to pull him down to her. "This is Christmas Day. Can't you love my baby because you love the Baby Jesus? Please forgive me. I have been good since I went away. Baby's father was good to us. I wanted you to come to see us and to learn to love him. He's dead, Daddy—dead —and baby and I are all alone in the world."

Still Enoch stood motionless, unable to speak.

"I want to see Mother," sobbed Martha. "Doesn't Mother love me and want to see me? O Daddy, I want you to care for me again. I want Mother to tell me how to make my baby grow to be like you. Please—please, take me home—even if I can only stay one night. I want to sleep in my own bed. I want Mother!"

Enoch winced. Martha wanted the baby to be like him, and he had been a demon for six years. How little Martha realized how her going had changed things. He looked sternly into her face and whispered, huskily:

"And Job?"

"Job?" questioned Martha. "I don't know where Job is. He took me only to Portland. He begged me not to go away; he tried to turn me back after we had started. Job has done you no wrong."

A GREAT load dropped from Enoch's mind as he listened to Martha's statement. He looked anxiously into her tired, loving, hungry eyes. He lifted her little body from the ground, kissing her passionately as he folded her close in his great arms, while the snowflakes fell fast about them.

For a moment both were silent; then she bent over and lifted the little baby, placing it in Enoch's arms, where she herself had been so glad to be.

"My Christmas present to you, Daddy!" she said. "Will you give little Enoch a home? I will try to be good if you will take me back."

"My own little Martha and her baby," said Enoch, as the tears rolled down his face. "Yes, I will love you, and your baby, dear. Come we will go home to Mother. She has never ceased to love you—to pray for you—to look for you."

"I've wanted you so, Daddy," said Martha, snuggling close to him. "I wanted to come home as soon as I had gone away. When my letter came back to me, I thought I couldn't live. I love the farm, and Mother, and you, Daddy. I loved my husband, and I love our baby."

ENOCH strapped the snowshoes on her feet, kissing her again and again as he helped her to her feet. He was so hungry for love after such a long time in the desert of loneliness. He lifted the baby into his arms, too full of emotion to speak, and they started for home.

Once more he had a baby boy—a boy to take the place of Benjamin. Martha had come home —and it was still Christmas. He struggled on ahead, trying to make a path for her. His heart was singing, as on that Christmas morning six years ago:

O come to my heart,
Lord Jesus,

There is room in my
heart for Thee.

"See, Daddy," cried Martha in a happy voice, "Mother is waiting. There is a light in the window for you."

"And for you, too, dear," added Enoch. "How Mother's eyes will shine when she sees the Christmas present you have brought her—and me! I want to watch her when you lay little Enoch in her arms. Martha, Mother has waited all day long to celebrate Christmas with me. We haven't had any at all yet. Indeed, she has waited patiently—more patiently than you will ever know—six long years—for a Christmas, and a Christmas present. Mother will be good to your baby; she will be glad to see you."

Enoch pressed a kiss on the face of the little boy in his arms and hurried on to take Martha, and God, and Christmas back to the farm house on the hillside.